GOLF *NOW!*

GOLF *NOW!*

Andrew Podnieks

FIREFLY BOOKS

A FIREFLY BOOK

Published by Firefly Books Ltd. 2008

First printing

Publisher Cataloging-in-Publication Data (U.S.)
Podnieks, Andrew.
     Golf Now! / Andrew Podnieks.
[176] p. : col. ill. ; cm.
Includes index.
Summary: Features golfer profiles and highlights the best and brightest competitors on the PGA and LPGA tours, including the Men's and Women's U.S. Open, The Masters, The British Open, the PGA and LPGA Championship.
ISBN-13: 978-1-55407-259-0 (pbk.)
ISBN-10: 1-55407-259-X (pbk.)
1. Golf -- Biography. 2. Professional Golfers Association.
I. Title.
796.352/ 092/2 dc22 GV964.A1.P636 2008

Library and Archives Canada Cataloguing in Publication
Podnieks, Andrew
     Golf now! / Andrew Podnieks.
Includes index.
ISBN-13: 978-1-55407-259-0
ISBN-10: 1-55407-259-X
     1. Golf--Biography. I. Title.
GV964.A1P63 2008   796.352092'2
C2007-904754-8

Published in the United States by
Firefly Books (U.S.) Inc.
P.O. Box 1338, Ellicott Station
Buffalo, New York 14205

Published in Canada by
Firefly Books Ltd.
66 Leek Crescent
Richmond Hill, Ontario L4B 1H1

Cover and interior design by Kimberley Young
Printed in China

The publisher gratefully acknowledges the financial support for our publishing program by the Government of Canada through the Book Publishing Industry Development Program.

PHOTO CREDITS

L = left, R = right, CL = center left, CR = center right, B = bottom

Reuters Images

Zainal Abd Halim 88; Jason Arnold 84 (B) (detail 5); Denis Balibouse 153; Carlos Barria 110; Shaun Best 6–7, 10, 21, 53, 63, 86, 87, 117, 145 (action images); Mike Blake 31, 52, 71, 82, 96, 107, 136, 144 (action images); Howard Burditt 112 (B) (detail 5); David Callow 37; Richard Carson 1, 108; Mike Cassese 3, 34 (L, CR), 38, 55, 136 (R), 139; Tami Chappell 148 (CR, B) (detail 5), 155, 156 (detail 148); Paul Childs/Action Images 66 (L), 80, 81, 94, 95, 112 (CL), 133; Tim Chong 152; Hans Deryk 36, 59, 158, 165; Jonathan Ernst 32, 34 (B) (detail 5), 62, 66 (R), 84 (L), 114; Mike Finn-Kelcey 69; Rick Fowler 3, 121, 166 (CL); Robert Galbraith 8 (CL), 16, 20, 24, 64, 66 (CL, B) (detail 5), 68, 72, 77, 84 (R), 89, 91, 93, 97, 98, 100, 119, 123, 124, 128, 131, 166 (B) (detail 5), 168 (detail 166), 170, 172 (detail 166); Hugh Gentry 46, 79, 90, 159 (detail 148); John Gress 39, 112 (L), 126, 127, 166 (CR); Lucas Jackson 34 (CL); Aaron Josefczyk 42, 66 (CR), 76; Chris Keane 26, 34 (R), 58, 118; Eddie Keogh 13, 154; Ron Kuntz 138, 173; Charles W. Luzier 18, 75, 112 (CR); Brandon Malone/Action Images 56, 57, 74, 132; David Moir 12, 73, 135, 148 (CL), 163; Max Morse 48, 49; Christinne Muschi 29; Yuriko Nakao 162, 164; Lucy Nicholson 140, 141; Phil Noble 8 (L), 11, 61; Alessia Pierdomenico 99, 102, 103, 106, 114; Frank Polich 92, 130; Jessica Rinaldi 19; Marc Serota 160; Tim Shaffer 157; Brian Snyder 2, 14, 22, 25, 33, 60, 111, 116, 122, 150, 161; John Sommers II 8 (R) 15, 30, 78, 83, 84 (CL, CR), 129, 136 (CR), 171; Aly Song 8 (CR); Darren Staples 43; Mike Stone 44, 45, 65, 120; Chaiwat Subprasom 134; Matt Sullivan 3, 8 (B) (detail 5), 17, 23, 28, 40, 41, 47, 70, 101, 109, 112 (R), 125; Jeff Topping 27; Jo Yong-Hak 151

Cover: Mike Cassese (*Vijay Singh*); Rick Fowler (*Phil Mickelson*); Kevin Lamarque (*Tiger Woods*); Danny Moloshok (*Lorena Ochoa*); Matt Sullivan (*Mike Weir*)

Back cover: Howard Burditt (*Padraig Harrington*); Jonathan Ernst (*K.J. Choi*); Robert Galbraith (*Sergio Garcia*); Yuriko Nakao (*Michelle Wie*); Brian Snyder (*Steve Stricker*)

Getty Images

Stephen Dunn, 51, 105; Sam Greenwood 104, 143 (PGA); Scott Halleran 50; Lecka 147 (detail 136); Hunter Martin 146; Redington 169; Jim Rogash 142 (detail 136)

CONTENTS

INTRODUCTION

*G*OLF NOW! captures the essence of the golfing world, profiling the top golfers on the PGA, the LPGA and around the world. It offers stories of how these great players came to dominate the game, provides vital statistics and career summaries, and even gives a glimpse into the under-appreciated world of the caddies, the people who not only carry the bags but often call the shots, select the clubs and read the breaks on the greens. If you love golf, this is the book for you. If you are new to the game, this is a terrific introduction to the top players of the sport.

In 2007, all of golf's protagonists played with a particular sense of drama. Phil Mickelson held off Tiger Woods to win the Deutsche Bank Challenge in September, a memorable mano-a-mano final pairing on the Sunday, which saw the left-hander Mickelson win by two strokes over Woods. Then there was Sergio Garcia at the British Open, standing on the 18th hole with a one-stroke lead and certain to win his first major — only to collapse. Mike Weir won in 2007 for the first time in more than three years, an October victory achieved after his remarkable win over Woods at the Presidents Cup in Montreal. Angel Cabrera won his first major, and young stars such as Zach Johnson and Justin Rose played their way to the top of the leaderboard with great consistency. Into the mix entered K.J. Choi, who won three times in '07. At the end of the year, though, it was Tiger Woods who was the focus, winning seven tournaments, the inaugural FedEx Cup, and the $10 million bonus that went with it. In 2007, Tiger became the youngest golfer to reach 60 career wins, and he added the PGA Championship to his majors' résumé, the 13th of his great career.

Also in 2007, women's golf continued its

explosion in popularity throughout the world, thanks in large part to the great achievements over the last decade of Swede Annika Sorenstam. While injuries cost Sorenstam most of 2007, Mexican Lorena Ochoa moved seamlessly into the number-one position. But Ochoa, the 2007 Player of the Year on the LPGA, must fend off a crop of young female stars, including Paula Creamer and Natalie Gulbis. Indeed, women's golf is more popular than ever before, notably in Asia where hero Se Ri Pak has made a remarkable impression.

The Tiger Woods era is now well into its second decade. But, of course, the rest of the golfing world is not about to surrender. There are too many great competitors for that. Indeed, the PGA Tour is blessed with an abundance of remarkable players from all over the world, and whenever Tiger plays, they are eager to try to beat him or, at the least, push him to the limit.

In fact, the cast of the PGA Tour reads like a novel full of drama and diverse international characters, all with one thing in common — a love for, and a supreme ability to play, the game called golf. First, there is Tiger Woods and his arch-enemy, fellow American Phil Mickelson, the number two player in the world, and a man who has defeated Woods more than once. There is Fijian Vijay Singh, another challenger and one who is not known for his friendship with Tiger on the course or off. Also in the mix are South African Ernie Els — the "Big Easy" — who has one of the most relaxed, perfect swings the game has ever known, the inscrutable Retief Goosen, also from South Africa, who can be one of the best in the world in any given week, and Irishman Padraig Harrington, the winner of the 2007 British Open. Meanwhile, Sergio Garcia from Spain, Tiger's supposed next big challenger, is still struggling for consistency. The drama continues....

The talent and shot-making of the men and women profiled in *GOLF NOW!* is perfectly summed up with the PGA Tour's ad campaign: These Guys Are Good.

Indeed, these players are very good.

Andrew Podnieks

CREAM
OF THE CROP

1

There are a great many incredibly skilled golfers in the world. Amazingly, though, there are only a small number who consistently play even better than the rest of the field. These golfers are the superstars of the game — the players who rarely succumb to pressure, the contenders at the biggest tournaments, the ones that other players watch on the leaderboard. These Cream of the Crop players are always the favorites, always the ones capable of mounting a charge on the final holes, the ones who can hold the putter with a steady hand with a tournament on the line.

Top (L-R): Mike Weir, Vijay Singh, Retief Goosen, Tiger Woods
Bottom: Phil Mickelson

Sure Chris DiMarco is a world-class golfer, like so many on the PGA Tour, but he stamped his place in golf history at the 2005 Presidents Cup. On a talented U.S. team stocked with players such as Tiger Woods, Phil Mickelson and Jim Furyk, it was the unassuming DiMarco who won four matches, halved a fifth, and sank a dramatic putt to clinch the championship for the Americans against the best from the rest of the world.

DiMarco was paired with Mickelson for fourball and foursomes matches — and they crushed their opponents — but it was DiMarco's singles match on Sunday against Stuart Appleby that was the clincher. In a close match, the two men arrived at the 18th green all square, but DiMarco drained a clutch birdie putt from 13 feet to win his match 1-up and give his team an insurmountable lead. He left the Robert Trent Jones Golf Club in Virginia a hero.

DiMarco's hero, in turn, was his mother, whose death in 2006 had a profound effect on him. He had organized the Norma DiMarco Tee Up for Life Tournament since 2001, which raised millions of dollars for charity in her name, and when she died of a heart attack in July 2006, Chris was devastated. Few moments were as poignant in golf as the medal ceremony of that year's British Open: A grieving DiMarco finished second only to Tiger Woods, whose father had recently died, and dedicated his tremendous performance to his mother; Tiger did the same for his father.

CAREER *HIGHLIGHTS*

Turned Pro: 1990

PGA Wins: 3

First PGA Win: 2000

Best Season-end Placing: 7th (2005)

Ryder Cup: 2

Presidents Cup: 2

Uses a "claw" grip to putt

Had just one top-10 finish in '07

Although his has been a steady presence on the PGA Tour for the last decade, DiMarco's fortunes were not so easily accomplished. He turned pro in 1990 and then bounced around lesser tours for several years before settling into the PGA. He started on the Nationwide Tour in 1991, moved to the Canadian Tour a year later, and earned his way back to the Nationwide in 1993. He had an excellent showing there and earned his PGA Tour card for '94. A good rookie season, though, gave way to a poor 1995, when he finished 174th on

the money list and got demoted right back to the Nationwide Tour. After another season there and on the Canadian Tour, DiMarco qualified for the PGA via Q-school at the end of 1997, and only then, after eight years in the minors, so to speak, did he go to the PGA for good.

It wasn't until 2000 that he finally won, though, that victory coming at the Pennsylvania Classic by six strokes. The event represented his 159th PGA tournament. He won again a year later at the Buick Challenge, defeating David Duval on the first playoff hole, and in 2002 he made it a hat trick by claiming first place at the Phoenix Open.

His most demoralizing loss came in 2004 at the Masters. Paired in the final group on Sunday with Phil Mickelson, the two men started the final round tied, but DiMarco shot a 76 and Mickelson pulled away from the field for the win. Between 2000 and 2005, DiMarco was in the top 20 of earnings every year, but the 2006 and 2007 seasons were tremendously disappointing.

On course, he is most easily recognized for his unique grip with the putter. Standing over the ball, he puts his top hand in position as might any golfer, and then he takes his bottom hand and turns it the other way so that his right thumb (of the lower hand) is almost touching the left thumb (of the upper). The grip allows him a more pendulum motion to his putting swing, and although unorthodox, it has given him confidence in the stroke he never had in his early years.

Like so many top-flight, world-class golfers, what is most amazing about DiMarco is that he hasn't won more often. His is a reliable and consistent game, yet nearly two decades after turning pro he has only three PGA wins, one on the Nationwide Tour, and one far away in Abu Dhabi. Both his incredible skill and moderate success speak to the final fact that winning in pro golf is extremely difficult. No matter. He will always be remembered for that thrilling Presidents Cup putt. ∎

ERNIE *ELS*

Born: Johannesburg, South Africa, October 17, 1969

On any given day, Ernie Els is, quite simply, the best golfer in the world. His career started in remarkable fashion and has been going strong ever since. Known as the "Big Easy" for his relaxed and perfectly-shaped swing, Els was a scratch golfer by the time he won the world under-14 championship. He turned pro at age 19 and has been among the world's best ball strikers ever since.

Els took his native South Africa by storm in 1992 when he became the first golfer since Gary Player to win the big three events in that country, namely the South African Open, the PGA and the Masters. The next year, Els became the first golfer ever to shoot four rounds in the 60s at the British Open, finishing in a tie for sixth place. The following year (1994), he made even greater strides, winning his first major at age 24 by finishing atop the leaderboard at the U.S. Open. He had a two-stroke lead going into the final round, but ended up in a playoff with Colin Montgomerie and Loren Roberts, winning on the second extra hole after the 18-hole playoff on Monday.

The next year, 1995, Els narrowly missed winning the PGA Championship, and in 1996 he won the World Match Play title for the third straight year. He was also the runner-up at the British Open. More than any other golfer of the modern era,

Els has combined success on the PGA Tour with success worldwide. In his early pro years on the PGA Tour, for instance, he also won tournaments in South Africa, Europe and Japan, flying from one continent to another while maintaining an energy and ability that defied jet lag.

Els made history in 1997 by winning his second U.S. Open, at the Congressional Country Club, becoming the first non-American to win the coveted event twice since Scotsman Alex Smith did it in 1906 and 1910. By 1998, Els was ranked the number-one player in the world and remained so for much of the summer.

While Tiger Woods was having a sensational season in 2000, Els was not far behind, having one of the greatest "second best" years in golf history. He was runner-up in the first three majors of the year — the Masters, the U.S. Open, the British Open — before finishing 34th in the final major, the PGA Championship. In all, he had five second-place finishes in 2000, as well as a win at the International, the tournament which uses the Stableford scoring system of points rather than the standard scoring system by strokes.

After a sub-par 2001 in which he failed to win on the PGA Tour — although he won the Players Championship in South Africa — Els bounced back with a brilliant year in 2002. He won his third and most recent major, the British Open, after a scare he almost paid dearly for. After 54 holes at Muirfield, Els led Soren Hansen by two strokes

CAREER *HIGHLIGHTS*

Turned Pro: 1989

PGA Wins: 15 (3 majors)

First PGA Win: 1994

Best Season-end Placing: 2nd (2004)

Ryder Cup: n/a

Presidents Cup: 5

Has won more than 40 times outside the PGA

Best finish in '07: 2nd at Verizon Heritage

and increased that lead to three with just eight holes to play. He faltered coming home, though, and had to go to a playoff with Steve Elkington, Thomas Levet and Stuart Appleby, surviving the four-hole playoff by being the only one to play in par. Els also won the Genuity Championship in the U.S., the Heineken Classic in Melbourne, the Dubai Desert Classic, the Cisco World Match Play title and the Nedbank Challenge.

Els came closest to performing the impossible in 2004 when he won the Order of Merit as top money winner in Europe while finishing an incredible ninth on the PGA's money list, a double level of success that is hard to fathom, given worldwide competition as well as travel. His career was halted in mid-flight in the summer of 2005, however, when he suffered a knee injury while sailing. The required surgery kept him out of action until the new year, and he struggled to regain confidence in his swing. A year later, though, he had put the injury out of his mind and produced another sensational season.

In 2007, Els had five top-5 finishes in 14 events, including a tie for fourth at the British Open and a third-place finish at the PGA Championship, in which he almost caught Tiger Woods over the final nine holes, finishing just three strokes behind. He also played in his fifth Presidents Cup and finished with a 3–2–0 record for the International squad.

Els has been one of very few golfers to admit publicly that he has been intimidated by Woods in various situations. Indeed, during his incredible career, he has finished second to Woods more than any other golfer on the PGA Tour and has rarely pushed Woods during the pressure of a final round of a big tournament. Els has had an astounding 26 top-10 finishes in his career at the majors, yet for a golfer of his extraordinary talent, it might be fair to say he has won "only" three major titles. He has won some 60 events worldwide and will go down as one of the greatest golfers of his era, an amazing ball-striker and a majestic talent. But "tremendous competitor" might be one epithet that he has not yet fully earned. ∎

His swing is as unorthodox as it is effective. His pre-shot routine is deliberate to the point of annoying. But Jim Furyk has been one of the most consistent and exceptional golfers for much of his 15-year career.

Fans can blame the swing on Furyk's father, Mike, the only swing coach Jim has ever had. It is a motion that would be difficult for any golfer to replicate and certainly not a motion any swing coach not named Furyk would espouse. It involves keeping the hands low and bringing the club up quickly and following through very high, almost in the manner of Kenny Perry. But for Furyk, the stroke works and that's all that matters.

Although Furyk didn't win during his first full season on the PGA Tour in 1994, he did make an impression by placing in the top 10 three times. The next year, he did, indeed, win — at the Las Vegas Invitational — thus starting a streak in which he won at least once in 11 of the next 13 years, through the 2007 season.

Furyk made his first big jump in 1997, when he had 13 finishes in the top 10 and placed fourth in money won. Despite not winning all season, he finished in the top 10 in three of the four majors that year, a 28th-place finish at the Masters his only blemish on an otherwise outstanding performance in the year's biggest events. He improved to third on the money list the next season and won the Las Vegas Invitational again to boost his earnings to over $2 million for the first time.

CAREER *HIGHLIGHTS*

Turned Pro: 1992

PGA Wins: 13 (1 major)

First PGA Win: 1995

Best Season-end Placing: 2nd (2006)

Ryder Cup: 5

Presidents Cup: 5

Only swing coach has been his father, Mike

Won 2007 Canadian Open

Along with his victories, Furyk is a model of consistency, missing precious few cuts every year and giving himself a chance to win every time out. In 1999 and 2000, he made 48 of 50 cuts and won at Las Vegas again (1999) as well as the Doral-Ryder Open (2000).

It was in 2003 that Furyk won his first and only major to date — the tough U.S. Open at Olympia Fields in Illinois. After three rounds in the 60s (67, 66, 67), Furyk had a three-stroke lead on the field to start the final day, and he managed to stave off charges from several challengers. His partner that day, Stephen Leaney, came close, but faltered down the stretch and finished second; Mike Weir had a great round going, but bogeyed the final two holes to finish third; and, Tiger Woods had a mini-rally snuffed out by a four-putt on the ninth green. In the end, Furyk's calm on

a course that turned treacherous on the final day earned him the win on Father's Day, appropriate given his relationship with his dad.

Despite that win, though, Furyk started the next season in frustrating fashion, suffering a wrist injury that required surgery, which limited him to just 14 tournaments in 2004. He made only eight cuts that year but came back strong in 2005 by winning in July at the Western Open and followed that with two narrow losses, one to Vijay Singh in a playoff at the Wachovia Championship and another to Padraig Harrington, who eagled the 72nd hole at the Barclays Classic to beat Furyk by a single stroke.

Furyk vaulted to number two in the world rankings in 2006 as his strong play reached a new level. He won twice and made 22 of 24 cuts. In 19 of those 22 tournaments in which he finished in the money, he placed among the top 25, a phenomenal stretch of high-level consistency. His 11 top-5 finishes led all golfers that year as well. His scoring average of 68.86 was also tops among players with 50 rounds or more on the year, earning him the Vardon Trophy for the lowest average score.

One of Furyk's victories in 2006 was the Canadian Open, and the following year he repeated as champion by firing a final-round 64. The 2007 tournament was being played for the first time the week after the British Open, yet despite the hectic schedule, Furyk bettered the field and won for the 13th time on tour.

In addition to his stroke play, Furyk has represented the U.S. in every Ryder and Presidents Cup since 1997. Most famously, he was 3–0–2 in 2005 and did what few golfers have been able to do in match play — pair up well with Tiger Woods. The Furyk-Woods team had a 2–0–1 record that year and was again a duo in 2007 when the U.S. dominated the International side in the Presidents Cup. Overall, Furyk has a great record at the Presidents Cup (13–9–2) and, oddly, a far less impressive one at the Ryder Cup (6–12–2). Regardless, he is at the top of his game now and is one of the top five golfers in the world, weird swing or not. ∎

RETIEF *GOOSEN*

Born: Pietersburg, South Africa, February 3, 1969

Reticent, quiet, dauntless and steely-nerved, Retief Goosen is so very close to becoming one of the greats of his generation, but he has yet to get there entirely. He has won tournaments all over the world, has a golf game without weakness and has won oodles of money, but he doesn't have the same crowd following as Tiger Woods; doesn't hammer the ball with John Daly-like excitement; and doesn't engage the fans quite like Phil Mickelson. And then, there's the lightning story.

Goosen started playing golf at age 11 in South Africa on the encouragement of his father, but at 16 he was struck by lightning while playing a round with friends. They had been on the course and took refuge during a storm. When the clouds cleared, they resumed play. Goosen walked after a drive on one hole that had found the trees, and while he was preparing to make his shot he was struck. He suffered burns; his clothes were singed and clubs scorched by the bolt; and, he was in such pain that he couldn't put on his shoes for days. It was only three weeks later that he started playing again, but it was much longer before he had recovered psychologically.

Goosen turned pro in 1990, shortly after winning the amateur championship of his country, and had almost immediate success in South Africa. He was Rookie of the Year in 1991, his first full season, and he won on the European Tour for the first time in 1996. Goosen moved to that Tour full-time and enjoyed similar success, even after 1999 when his season was shortened after he broke his arm in a skiing accident.

In 2000, Goosen started to play on the PGA with greater frequency, and the next year he enjoyed double success in America and Europe. In the latter, he won the Order of Merit, and in

the former, he won the U.S. Open in just his 38th PGA start. Goosen needed 90 holes of golf to achieve that win after he and Mark Brooks were tied at the end of 72 holes. The tie came after a disastrous final hole in which Goosen three-putted at the 18th hole on Sunday to surrender the lead at Southern Hills Country Club. On Monday, he beat Brooks 70–72.

Despite the rigors of travel, Goosen continued to play worldwide, and in 2002 he again won the European Order of Merit while finishing 10th on the PGA list. He won the BellSouth Classic in the U.S., and with that moved into fourth place in the world rankings. It was in 2004, though, that he earned a place in the history books by winning his second U.S. Open on a wild final day at Shinnecock Hills.

Goosen led Phil Mickelson and Ernie Els at the start of the final day, but he relinquished the lead in the early going, and as he stood on the 16th tee, he trailed Mickelson by a shot. Fate intervened again, though, as Mickelson double-bogeyed the 17th and Goosen birdied the 16th. Goosen stayed calm on the final two holes to win by a stroke.

A year later, though, when the 2005 Open moved to Pinehurst No. 2, Goosen failed horribly in his attempt to win consecutive U.S. Opens. He was leading the field by three strokes after 54 holes. His nearest rivals were Jason Gore and Olin Brown, two journeymen who could not possibly have posed any psychological threat to Goosen's preparations for that final round. Yet Goosen went out and shot a +11 score of 81 and finished in 11th spot, eight shots behind winner Michael Campbell.

Despite this lapse, Goosen enjoyed a tremendous 2005, winning in America and Europe again and posting a remarkable 4–0–1 record at the Presidents Cup, including a brilliant 2-and-1 win over Tiger Woods in their singles match on Sunday. In the four majors, Goosen was the best performer all year, even though he didn't win one of the four most important championships. He tied for 3rd at the Masters, tied for 11th at the U.S. Open, tied for 5th at the British Open, and tied for 6th at the PGA Championship.

CAREER *HIGHLIGHTS*

Turned Pro: 1990

PGA Wins: 6 (2 majors)

First PGA Win: 2001

Best Season-end Placing: 6th (2004)

Ryder Cup: n/a

Presidents Cup: 4

Career put on hold after being struck by lightning as a teenager

Tied for 2nd at the 2007 Masters tournament

The 2006 and 2007 seasons were slightly less kind to Goosen. He didn't win on the PGA Tour in that time, and his success overseas was also limited. But his game is too good and his makeup too strong to prevent him from winning again and often. In all, he has won six times in the U.S. and 21 times in other parts of the world, from Europe to Asia to South Africa. The burns he suffered as a teenager might have singed his skin, but they didn't destroy his resolve to become a world-class golfer. Goosen is the real deal, and a golfer who can play with Tiger, Phil and Ernie any day of the week. ■

PHIL *MICKELSON*

Born: San Diego, California, June 16, 1970

For the longest time, Phil Mickelson was dubbed by the media as "the best player never to have won a major." When he finally did, in 2004, he got rid of a demon that had long haunted him. In all, Mickelson is the finest left-handed golfer in the sport's history and has been one of the top five golfers for more than a decade.

Such has been the consistently high level of play Mickleson has brought to his game that, even as a teen, he put his name among the elite. For instance, he became only the third golfer to win the U.S. Amateur and NCAA Championship in the same year. The other two? Jack (as in Nicklaus) and Tiger (as in Woods). To this day, Mickelson is the last amateur to win a PGA Tour event, a feat he accomplished in 1991 at the Northern Telecom Open.

These early results were not youthful excursions to heights unknown; they were merely signs of things to come. In 1994, his first full year on tour, Mickelson won twice and finished 22nd on the money list. During his first six years, he won 12 times and rose to the top by virtue of playing under pressure better than most of the field.

Yet everything about Mickelson's career can be divided into pre-2004 and post-2004. The earlier incarnation was a wild swinger. Mickelson was a long hitter, famous for pulling out his driver on every long hole and hitting the ball as far as he could. Direction and accuracy seemed unimportant to him, and the results often proved disastrous. Time and again he refused to play conservatively, when a mid-distance shot off the tee to the middle of the fairway would have sufficed. Just as often, he took what should have been an easy par and turned it into a bogey or double bogey after an errant drive.

In 2004, Mickelson learned to compromise. He had heard the insults from Butch Harmon, Tiger Woods's coach, who lambasted the lefty for being obsessed with distance, not accuracy, off the tee. The result was a golfer who controlled the ball better, controlled his stroke better, and managed the course with greater intelligence. At that year's Masters in Augusta, Georgia, Mickelson and Chris DiMarco were tied after 54 holes, and as

CAREER *HIGHLIGHTS*

Turned Pro: 1992

PGA Wins: 32 (3 majors)

First PGA Win: 1991

Best Season-end Placing: 2nd (2000–02)

Ryder Cup: 6

Presidents Cup: 7

Three career majors an all-time best for lefties

Won three times in 2007, notably the Players Championship

win. Mickelson later finished third at the British Open to cap the finest season of his career.

To prove the Masters win was no fluke, Mickelson won majors in 2005 and 2006 as well. In 2005, he won the PGA Championship, and then the next year he captured his second green jacket at Augusta National, besting Tim Clark by two strokes.

But just as it seemed Mickelson was getting used to winning the big events, he threw one away. Standing at the tee of the final hole of the 2006 U.S. Open, he led the tournament by one stroke. His drive went well left and fell in among a clump of trees, but instead of just chipping the ball out to the fairway, he tried to reach the green with his second shot. The ball hit a tree and fell near where he stood. His third shot fell short of the green, his chip was not close, and two putts later he had given the tournament away to Geoff Ogilvy. So shocked and disgusted was he that Mickelson packed his clubs, went home, and didn't play again that year.

Everyone was anxious to see how Mickelson would play in 2007. In truth, he recovered fully from the devastation of that 2006 U.S. Open loss. He won quickly to start 2007, taking the AT&T Pebble Beach tournament in February and the next week lost the Nissan Open in a playoff. He then won the Players Championship. But midway through 2007, he suffered a painful wrist injury that hampered his play. He ended the year strongly, though, by beating Tiger Woods on the final day of the Deutsche Bank Championship, his best performance of the year. In September, he teamed effectively with Woody Austin at the Presidents Cup in Montreal and earned three points for the U.S.

Mickelson has remained among the best of the best for most of his career, and now that he has proved he can win a major, he has solidified his place in the game's history. The only questions left are how many more majors can he win and how often can he battle Tiger Woods successfully? The two have never been the best of friends, but this has made golf only more exciting. Mickelson isn't done yet. ■

the final day wore on, DiMarco faded and Ernie Els entered the picture. Standing over an 18-foot birdie putt on the 72nd hole, Mickelson was tied with Els and a playoff seemed likely. Then, Mickelson drained the putt, jumped inches in the air (as players joked later), and got the biggest monkey off his back. He was no longer the best player to have never won a major. It took him 47 tries, but he finally won the big one!

Weeks later, he almost won the U.S. Open, but his double bogey at the 17th hole on Sunday allowed Retief Goosen to sneak past him for the

VIJAY *SINGH*

Born: Lautoka, Fiji, February 22, 1963

Singh is legendary among caddies for his no-nonsense work ethic and extremely long, hard hours on the driving range, while he is also considered by some golfers to be genial with a great sense of humor. There is, however, an apocryphal story that speaks to Vijay Singh's dual personalities: Meeting Tiger Woods at the first tee of the final round of a tournament several years ago, the two great golfers in the final pairing, Tiger extended a hand and said, "Good luck." To which Singh rejoined, "Titleist 7," in reference only to the ball he would be playing.

Although Singh turned pro in 1982, he didn't have much of an impact on the game for another decade. He was for years a club pro in Borneo and an itinerant golfer in Europe and Africa, but when he decided to focus on the PGA in 1993, he wasted no time in establishing himself as a great player. He won the Buick Classic and was named Rookie of the Year that first season, but his sophomore season was marred by neck and back trouble that limited his effectiveness.

From 1993 to 1997, Singh won five times in the U.S. and another seven times abroad. He earned a reputation for a smooth swing and excellent iron shots, but it was the practice routines that made him the stuff of legend. He would go right from the 18th green of a tournament to the driving range and stay until dark, and arrive hours before his tee time to work on his short game. Additionally, he routinely played more tournaments in a season than any of the other top names in the game. His devotion to the game paid off.

In 1998, Singh had seven top-10 finishes in 24 events, and the next year he won his first major. He won the PGA Championship at Sahalee with a two-stroke win over Steve Stricker, and he won his second major two years later at the Masters. His only other major came at the 2004 PGA Championship.

In fact, 2004 produced a career year for Singh in many ways. That win at the PGA was accomplished with a final round 76, the highest score on a Sunday to win a major since 1938. Soon after, he beat Tiger Woods and Adam Scott in the closing holes of the Deutsche Bank Championship to overtake Woods as the number-one golfer according to world rankings. It was his sixth win of the year and was

CAREER *HIGHLIGHTS*

Turned Pro: 1982

PGA Wins: 31 (3 majors)

First PGA Win: 1993

Best Season-end Placing: 1st (2003–04)

Ryder Cup: n/a

Presidents Cup: 7

"Vijay" means "victory" in Hindi

Won the Mercedes-Benz Championship to start 2007

followed a week later by win number seven, this at the Canadian Open, when he beat Mike Weir in a playoff. In all, Singh finished the year with the most victories of anyone — nine — and became the first golfer ever to win $10 million in a season. His 18 top-10 finishes were also the best, and he was named Player of the Year at age 41.

Singh has hardly let up. In 2005, he won four more times, finishing second on the money list with more than $8 million in earnings. During this time, he regained his number-one position for several weeks. Again, he had an incredible 18 top-10 finishes. The next year, Singh won only once, but for the third straight year achieved that 18-time, top-10 statistic — a testament to his consistency and dedication. Yet, while his relationship with Tiger Woods might be, at best, professional, Singh owes it to his adversary for pushing him. A significant part of Singh's late-career success is due to his fitness regimen of the last few years, which has enabled him to maintain his stamina at a time when many golfers fade quietly into the sunset. The regime, for Singh and for many other golfers, came in response to Woods's meticulous conditioning.

In 2007, Singh, at 44, won two more tourn-aments and had several top-10 finishes, and came second (behind Woods) in yearly earnings. Singh won the first event of the year, the Mercedes Benz Championship, and 10 weeks later won the Arnold Palmer Invitational. He qualified again for the Presidents Cup team, for the seventh straight year. Singh has but a 14–15–6 record in that prestigious event, however. He lost to Fred Couples 1-up in the final round of the 2005 event and in 2007, partnered variously with Mike Weir and Stuart Appleby, could muster only a 2–2–1 record.

Despite his spectacular career, Singh is not a spectacular player. He is a long hitter as opposed to short, but by no means a giant off the tee. He is perhaps more comfortable with the driver than any golfer on tour, however, and will never keep it in his bag when a hole has the length to require its use. Singh has been for years a proponent of the belly putter, though he will occasionally return to the standard-size club when he isn't putting well. Most of all, he is consistent and unflappable under pressure. He, along with Mickelson, Els and Goosen form that small group of players who are always the greatest challengers to Tiger Woods. Singh, as much as any, claims his fair share of the glory. ∎

MIKE *WEIR*

Born: Bright's Grove, Ontario, May 12, 1970

For one week in September 2004, Mike Weir carried the hopes and dreams of a nation on his back, and he came within one putt of giving Canada what it desperately wanted — a champion of its own for its national tournament, the Canadian Open.

Weir played brilliantly to open the tournament, firing a 68 and then 65 to head into the weekend at Glen Abbey with a chance to become the first Canadian since Pat Fletcher in 1954 to win at home. He was paired with Cliff Kresge for the final round, but just one group ahead were Jesper Parnevik and Vijay Singh. Kresge and Parnevik faded, but Singh charged, and Weir faltered just enough to give Singh a chance.

Heading up the 18th fairway, Weir needed a birdie to win and par to force a playoff with Singh, who finished at –9. Weir sent his approach shot into a greenside bunker and ended with a par. On the first playoff hole, the 18th, both he and Singh made birdie, and on the second hole, the 17th, Weir had a fantastic chance to win when Singh missed his par putt. But Weir, too, slid his putt past the hole to force a third hole, and this time Singh prevailed as Weir put his second shot in the water. It was an outstanding tournament for Weir, but not the finish he, and the millions of fans across Canada, had been looking forward to all day.

Weir has become the most successful Canadian golfer of all time. He has eight PGA Tour victories and has won more than $15 million in a career that began in 1992 when he turned pro. In 2003, he won the Masters, the first Canadian to win a major. It was a fitting reward for a man who took six years of qualifying to earn his Tour card, which he did in 1998, after living out of his car and playing the Canadian and Nationwide Tours to earn a meager living.

The Masters victory, won in a playoff over Len Mattiace, showcased Weir's greatest asset: his ability to make middle-distance pressure putts. Time and again he holed those nerve-racking eight-foot putts for par or birdie, most notably on the 72nd hole to force a playoff. Weir's final round was bogey-free, the first time since 1957 a winner played errorless on the last day, and he beat Mattiace by sinking a bogey putt on the first extra hole to win Canada's first green jacket.

As a result of this success, the expectations and demands on his time proved a strain on Weir in 2004. He won the Nissan Open, and finished in the top 10 in two majors — tied for fourth at the U.S. Open and ninth at the British Open. But he missed the cut six times in the 22 events he entered and his earnings dropped to $2.7 million.

CAREER *HIGHLIGHTS*

Turned Pro: 1992

PGA Wins: 8 (1 major)

First PGA Win: 1999

Best Season-end Placing: 5th (2003)

Ryder Cup: n/a

Presidents Cup: 4

First lefty to win the Masters (2003)

Re-built his swing at the start of 2007

In spite of this, he was 14th on the money list and maintained his sixth-place world ranking.

Then came the struggles which seemed to have no end. His world ranking dropped, and the poorer his results, the worse his confidence. The downward spiral continued to the breaking point. In the winter of 2006, he changed swing coaches and revamped his swing entirely, a decision that could only be made with long-term commitment and a knowledge that the process would be measured in years, not weeks.

Indeed, Weir's 2007 season was a highly disappointing one for the first eight months — and then something happened. Although he made the cut in most of the tournaments he entered, he finished well down the final leaderboard almost every week and rarely challenged for a win on Sunday. He became the center of a controversy later in the year when the International team's captain Gary Player selected Weir for the Presidents Cup team despite Weir not having played well enough to earn a spot on the team

(the September 2007 event was being held for the first time in Canada).

Yet Weir rose to the occasion, proved Player a sage for his decision, and gave Canadians memories that will last a lifetime. To be sure, Weir and the Internationals were beaten handily by the U.S., 19½ to 14½, but Weir earned 3½ points for his side, most notably a full point on the final day by beating Tiger Woods in singles play on the ultimate hole. The roar of the gallery as Tiger conceded the 18th hole and the match was spine-tingling, and that day will go down as one of the greatest games in Canadian golfing history.

Weir parlayed this emotional success into greater personal victory just a month later when he won the Fry's Electronics Open by a stroke over Mark Hensby, Weir's first win on tour in more than three years. It had been a long and arduous road from 2004 to 2007, but Weir felt his sacrifice was worth it, and no doubt, as he continues to hit stride with his new swing, greater things are in store for 2008 and beyond. ∎

In 2006, Tiger Woods played in 19 tournaments. He made the cut in every one, finished in the top 10 an amazing 14 times, won once, and earned more than $5.3 million to finish fourth on the money list. For just about any other golfer, this would have been a career year; for Woods, it was very much an off year that served to motivate him even more.

A career year? Try the year 2000, when Woods won the British Open, the U.S. Open and the PGA Championship, and then won the 2001 Masters to become the first golfer ever to hold all four majors! Woods lost his status as number-one player on tour in 2004, to Vijay Singh, but only after a record 332 weeks as the top golfer on the planet. He ended 2004 by continuing arguably the greatest streak in golf, having made each of the past 133 cuts, a record that might be as hard to break as Dimaggio's 56-game hitting streak or Gretzky's 92 goals in a season. The streak ended in 2005 when he missed the cut by a single stroke at the Byron Nelson Championship after 142 cuts made over seven years.

Woods burst onto the golfing scene at the age of two. Yes, two. That's how old he was when he putted with Bob Hope on the *Mike Douglas Show*. A year later, he shot 48 for nine holes, and at age five he was profiled in *Golf Digest*. His dad, Earl, called him Tiger in honor of a Vietnamese soldier friend Earl had met while serving in Vietnam. To everyone else, however, the name Tiger symbolizes the single-minded tenacity that he brings to the golf course every day, every shot.

By the time Woods turned pro in 1996, he had become the first player ever to win three straight U.S. amateur titles. He not only brought a superior game to the PGA — he also brought a superior attitude. He worked out every day, lifting weights, training in the gym and eating healthily. If golfers were going to keep up with him, they would have to do the same, and to their credit and his, many have.

Woods won two tournaments as a rookie and has never failed to win at least once a year, every year since. It was in his sophomore year of 1997, though, that he established himself as a player vastly superior to everyone else. His four-day score of 270 at the Masters was a tournament record,

Turned Pro: 1996

PGA Wins: 61 (13 majors)

First PGA Win: 1996

Best Season-end Placing: 1st (1997, 1999–2002, 2005–07)

Ryder Cup: 5

Presidents Cup: 5

Youngest player ever to win 13 majors and 50 PGA events

Won seven times in 2007, including the PGA Championship

and he won by a colossal margin — 12 strokes — also a record. In 1998, Woods won eight tournaments in one season, and in '99 he won four successive tournaments, a feat previously accomplished in 1953 by Ben Hogan.

It was the year 2000, though, that will go down as possibly his greatest achievement. He entered 20 tournaments that year, and finished under par in every one! His three majors completed the career Grand Slam, and at 24 he became the youngest player ever to achieve the legendary feat.

But as much as the winning was impressive, it was the *margin* of victory that was staggering. At the U.S. Open, Woods won by a ridiculous 15 strokes. At the British Open, his –19 was the best score in relation to par in the history of major championship play. He won the Canadian Open in his first try, sealing the victory with one of the greatest shots the game has ever seen: a 218-yard iron from a fairway bunker, over water, that landed 20 feet from the pin.

Woods has already won 13 majors, trailing only Jack Nicklaus (with 18) as the all-time winningest golfer in the ultimate tests. None of Woods's wins

was more profound than his British Open title in 2006. He had missed the cut at the U.S. Open earlier in the year, the first time he failed to qualify for weekend play as a pro in the majors, but that was because he was playing for the first time since the death of his father. After tapping in for the win at the Royal Liverpool in July, however, he broke down and hugged his caddy, Steve Williams, the emotions of his first win without his father too much to conceal.

In 2007, Woods continued to maintain his status as the world's greatest golfer. He won 5 of 13 tournaments he entered, including the PGA Championship, which was his first win as a father. His wife Elin had recently given birth to a girl, Sam, and Woods promptly went out and proved to the world that fatherhood might make him a different man, but not a less successful golfer. He also played in his fifth straight Presidents Cup, returning to Canada for the first time since winning the Canadian Open seven years before.

Woods has been the number-one golfer for so long, it is clear his very destiny is to be called the greatest of all time. He will surely break Nicklaus's record for major wins, will surely win more tournaments than anyone else in the game's history, and will surely leave a legacy the likes of which might never be equaled in the ancient game's glorious history. ∎

TOUR
VERTERANS

2

Earning a PGA Tour card is one thing, but keeping it and playing at a world-class level year after year is another matter altogether. Tour Veterans are just those players. They are the ones who always make the top 125 on the money list, the ones who earn special exemptions through their exceptional play, the ones who are most likely to challenge or defeat any one of the Cream of the Crop. Golf is a game that sees the top golfers mature in their thirties and play high-caliber golf well into their forties. But it's the Tour Veterans who usually play serious golf up to and sometimes beyond their 50th birthday, when they become eligible to play in the Champions Tour.

Top (L-R): Stephen Ames, Steve Stricker, Trevor Immelman, Rory Sabbatini
Bottom: K.J. Choi

ROBERT *ALLENBY*

Born: Melbourne, Australia, July 12, 1971

Although Robert Allenby's success in North America is limited to two excellent years — 2000 and 2001 — he has been among the world's leading golfers since turning pro in 1991, thanks to his additional success in Europe and in his home country, Australia. Not made of superstar material, he is nonetheless an efficient and consistent player at the elite level.

Allenby's rise through the ranks has been steady and impressive. As a rookie in Australia, he won the 1991 Riversdale Cup, a tournament he had won the previous year as an amateur. In his first full season as a pro in 1992, he led the Australasian Order of Merit and was named Rookie of the Year. After that, he only got better.

Allenby won the Order of Merit again two years later (1994) and played in his first Presidents Cup at age 23 at the Robert Trent Jones Golf Club in Virginia. He had a 1–3 record, losing a close final 1-up to Hale Irwin. By 1996, he had moved on to the more challenging European Tour and wasted no time in rising to the challenge. Allenby won three times that year and finished third on the Order of Merit. Wins included the Alamo English Open, the Peugeot French Open and the British Masters. All the while, he played a modest number of events in North America, but his success was even more modest — only a handful of cuts made and low weekend finishes.

Allenby also played in the 1996 Presidents Cup, posting a 2–3 record, which included a bad 6-and-5 loss to Steve Stricker in the singles matches on Sunday. But by 1998, he believed he was ready to tackle the PGA Tour, and to that end he went to Q-school at the end of '98 to try his luck. He finished 17th at the grueling six-round event, good enough to earn his full Tour card for the following season. He finished 126th on the money list that year, but still managed to play 26 events in 2000, his first of two career seasons.

CAREER *HIGHLIGHTS*

Turned Pro: 1991

PGA Wins: 4

First PGA Win: 2000

Best Season-end Placing: 16th (2000–01)

Ryder Cup: n/a

Presidents Cup: 4

In winning twice in 2000, Allenby took the hard way each time, earning the victories in a playoff on both occasions. In the first, he beat Craig Stadler in a four-hole playoff at the Houston Open. In the second, he bettered Nick Price on the first extra hole of the Western Open. Allenby ended his excellent season by going home and winning the Australian PGA Championship.

Weeks later, he started his second full year on the PGA and won his third career title in an incredible six-man playoff at the Nissan Open. Allenby was the only man to birdie the first extra hole, giving him a perfect 3–0 record in playoffs on the PGA and an 8–0 record worldwide. He won the Pennsylvania Classic later in the year and finished 16th on the money list for the second straight year.

Although Allenby hasn't won on the PGA since those two events in 2001, he has hardly been unsuccessful or idle. He made history in 2005 by winning Australia's "triple crown," claiming the titles of the Australian Open, PGA, and Masters in consecutive weeks, the first man to do so.

In 2007, Allenby started his year in a style which spoke to his 2000-2001 form, placing in the top 10 in six of his first eight events. Yet for all his 19 worldwide victories, his performance in the big tournaments has been uninspired at best. In 46 career majors, he has missed the cut 19 times, including the first three of 2007. His best finish was a tie for 12th at the 2002 U.S. Open. His Presidents Cup record continued to be weak as well. In 2000, he was 0–4, and in 2003, it was a moderate 2–2. Strange that the man with a 8–0 record in playoffs can do so poorly in the big-time moments of match-play golf. Still, Allenby has the game, so no one will be surprised if one day he wins a major and joins the honor roll of the truly great players of all time. ∎

The life and career of Stephen Ames has been complicated by two aspects of his character and personality which have come to define his reputation. First, since immigrating to Canada from Trinidad, he has become one of only two Canadians who compete at the highest level on a weekly basis, thus ensuring extra pressure from fans to do as well as fellow Canadian, Mike Weir. Second, there is Ames's relationship with Tiger Woods, which has become one of controversy and intrigue. But at the end of the day there is one thing no one can deny Ames — that he is the 2006 Players Championship winner. As golf's unofficial fifth major, this is a boast that few men can equal.

Ames has become a true world-class golfer over the course of several years' hard work. He turned pro in 1987 in his native Trinidad and played there and in Europe for several years, as well as on the

Nationwide Tour in the early 1990s. His career year in 2006 was followed with a disappointing 2007. As a result, he missed a chance to add to his international résumé, as he was passed over for selection to the International team for the 2007 Presidents Cup. Mike Weir was the lone Canadian representative at the tournament, which was held in Canada for the first time.

Ames's 2006 season didn't start as though it would be his career year. In fact, early on he made a comment that some might consider to be golf suicide. The remark was made leading up to his first-round match with Tiger Woods at the World Match Play Championship. Simply put, Ames said that because of Woods's erratic hitting off the tee, that the great Tiger was perfectly beatable in a match play event. Ames lost 9-and-8, the most lop-sided loss in tournament history. Point made; point taken.

CAREER *HIGHLIGHTS*

Turned Pro: 1987

PGA Wins: 3

First PGA Win: 2004

Best Season-end Placing: 8th (2004)

Ryder Cup: n/a

Presidents Cup: 0

Yet Ames was not cowed, nor did he apologize for his words. He had spoken as he saw it, and he was wrong. End of story. Two weeks later, he finished in a tie for seventh at the Honda Classic to make clear he was not psychologically devastated by the terrible loss to Tiger.

Indeed, by the time Ames got to TPC Sawgrass in Florida in 2006 for the Players Championship, his game was in great shape. He fired a 71 and 66 on the first two days of the tournament to make the cut and give himself a chance, and his 70 on Saturday brought him a little closer to the leaders. Still, neither he nor those in front of him could have anticipated what transpired on the final day. For starters, TPC Sawgrass is famous above all for its "island hole," the par-3 17th, which is short but whose green is surrounded by water. Tournaments are won or lost at this hole, and nerves are frayed all day in dreaded anticipation of having to play it in order to get to the clubhouse. On this weekend, though, Ames didn't allow the hole to get the better of him, and he hit the green all four days of the tournament.

On the final day, the scoring average shot up above 75 on the par 72 course. Incredibly, Ames shot a low round of 67 to win by a whopping six shots over Retief Goosen, his nearest rival. It was a win marked by brilliant approach shots after reliable, accurate, and altogether unspectacular tee shots. In short, it was a typical round of golf for Ames, and on this day it gave him the biggest win of his career.

The victory was worth $1.44 million to Ames,

the largest purse on the Tour, and it put him in the top 10 on the money list for 2006, automatically giving him an invitation to the Masters a few weeks later. He found himself in an awkward situation: On the one hand, his wife was recovering from lung cancer, and the family had planned a vacation for that week; on the other hand, the Masters doesn't happen every day. So, the Ames clan changed their plans, and he finished in an excellent 11th place in Augusta, Georgia, to continue his fine season.

Despite a disappointing 2007, Ames finished on a high note, winning the Children's Miracle Network Classic, the final event of the season. His −17 total was a stroke better than Tim Clark's and launched Ames to 31st on the year-end money list with over $2 million in earnings. Ames's only other Tour win came back in 2004 at the Western Open in Illinois.

Canadian or not, Ames has steadily worked his way into the upper echelon of golfers through hard work and competitive spirit, qualities he will need to maintain for long-term success. ■

If it weren't for Tiger Woods, K.J. Choi might well have been named the golfer of the year for 2007. He won two tournaments that year, added five other top-10 finishes to his résumé, won more than $5 million, and finished in the top five of the money list. It was, to be sure, a career year for Kyoung-Ju Choi.

Choi turned professional in his homeland of South Korea in 1994 and struck out to see the world through golf at age 24. He didn't make it to the PGA until 2000, however, honing his swing on the European and Asian Tours for several years first. Choi won four times in Korea before the turn of the 21st century, but since earning his PGA Tour card through Q-school at the end of 1999, he has lived in Houston, Texas, and focused most of his time and energy on the premier American tour.

Choi finished outside the top 125 (for automatic PGA qualification) by the end of his rookie season (2000) and was forced back to Q-school, but he earned his card the hard way and got back into life on the PGA for 2001. That season, he made 19 of 29 cuts and finished 65th in earnings, proving in his own mind he could handle the PGA and ensuring he had seen the last of qualifying.

It was during his third season (2002) that

CAREER *HIGHLIGHTS*

Turned Pro: 1994

PGA Wins: 6

First PGA Win: 2002

Best Season-end Placing: 5th (2007)

Ryder Cup: n/a

Presidents Cup: 2

Choi, more commonly called "The Tank" because of his fiercely competitive nature, and his short, stocky build, made his first breakthrough by winning twice and moving into the top echelon of players. He won the Compaq Classic of New Orleans by four strokes, becoming only the fourth Asian player to win on tour after Isao Aoki, Shigeki Maruyama and T.C. Chen. A short time later, Choi led from start to finish to capture the Tampa Bay Classic. In all, he won more than $2 million and finished 17th on the money list. As a result of his fine season, Choi was selected by captain Gary Player to join the International side at the 2003 Presidents Cup. Choi had a respectable 2–2 record, including a fine 4-and-2 win over Justin Leonard on the final day of singles play.

After a two-year drought, Choi won once in 2005 and again in 2006, but it was 2007 that stands out as his crowning glory. He won the Memorial Tournament in June, the signature event hosted by Jack Nicklaus at the Muirfield Village Golf Club, by coming from five strokes back on the final day and shooting a 65 for the win. It was a significant moment for Choi to receive the trophy from Nicklaus because it was a book by Nicklaus that Choi had used as a boy in South Korea to learn about the game and which had inspired him to become a pro.

A month after the Memorial Tournament, Choi struck for another win, the sixth of his career, at another famous player's tournament. He won the AT&T National, the inaugural event hosted by Tiger Woods, after firing a final-round

68 to beat Steve Stricker by three strokes. With the win, Choi also ensured his spot on the 2007 Presidents Cup team and a high placing at the year-end FedEx playoff.

Through his successes of 2007, Choi has established himself as a consistent and formidable golfer. He has had only two top-10 finishes in the majors, though (3rd at the 2004 Masters and a tie for eighth at the 2007 British Open), but as he nears his 40th birthday, he seems to be reaching full stride and playing with a confidence he has never previously enjoyed.

Part of that confidence comes from his caddy, Andy Prodger. Their first tournament together was the German Masters in 2003, and Choi won that event. They began a full-time partnership at the aforementioned 2004 Masters, and Prodger, who started with Nick Price during that great player's prime, has been with Choi ever since. ∎

STEWART CINK

Born: Huntsville, Alabama, May 21, 1973

Stewart Cink is the poster boy for the Nationwide Tour, the very reason the "farm team" Tour exists. He wasted no time in getting to the PGA Tour, but he did it the hard way — he earned it.

Cink graduated from Georgia Tech in 1995 after being named the top college golfer in the U.S. in his final year. He started on the Nationwide Tour that year, playing in just three events and making only one cut. As well, through special invitations and exemptions, he played five times on the PGA Tour, making four cuts and earning enough money to rank an impressive 192nd. Then in 1996, Cink tore the Nationwide Tour apart, setting a record with earnings of $251,699. He won three tournaments, led the Tour in money won, and was named Player of the Year. He also earned his PGA Tour card as a result. The top Nationwide graduate has never looked back.

Cink earned a win in his first full season on the PGA Tour (1997). He put himself in contention at the Greater Hartford Open but was still five shots back to start the final round. He then shot a flawless 66 for a one-stroke victory over three players. In all, he had a second-place finish and two other top-10 placings, finished 29th on the money list, and was named Rookie of the Year, the first player ever to win Player of the Year honors on the Nationwide Tour and Rookie of the Year on the PGA Tour in successive seasons.

Although he had a solid but unspectacular 1999 season, Cink came back in 2000 with another series of excellent finishes. He won for the second time, this at the MCI Classic. He birdied three of the last four holes to beat Tom Lehman by two strokes, and his steady play all year earned him a spot on the Presidents Cup team for the

CAREER HIGHLIGHTS

Turned Pro: 1995

PGA Wins: 4

First PGA Win: 1997

Best Season-end Placing: 5th (2004)

Ryder Cup: 3

Presidents Cup: 3

U.S. Cink responded by winning all four matches he played, including a pressure-filled 2-and-1 win over Greg Norman on the final day of singles matches. It was Cink's first taste of international match-play golf and he shone.

Cink was back in the spotlight in 2002, playing at the Ryder Cup. Fate was not so kind to him, or his teammates, this time round, and Cink lost all three matches he played. In the 2004 Ryder Cup, he earned 3½ points for the Americans, but this was during an 18½ to 9½ drubbing by the Europeans, so Cink's personal successes were understandably overshadowed by the lopsided defeat. The same happened in 2006 at the Ryder Cup when Cink and his teammates managed to put up little opposition in a one-sided European win. He made amends at the Presidents Cup in 2007, however, compiling an impressive 3-1-0 record in the Americans' dominating victory.

For the last 11 years, Cink has been a staple on the PGA Tour and has never finished lower than 73rd on the money list. His best year was 2004, when he was fifth on the list with earnings of more than $4.4 million. He won twice that year and was named to his second Ryder Cup team. His first win since 2000 came at the MCI Heritage, the same tournament he had won four years earlier. This time, he set a Tour record by winning after trailing by nine strokes through 54 holes. He shot a 64 on Sunday and then beat Ted Purdy on the fifth playoff hole for the win. Later in the season, he led from start to finish to win the World Golf Championships.

Despite Cink's international match-play experience and his success on both the Nationwide Tour and PGA Tour, he hasn't performed well at majors. His best showing came in 2001 when he finished in third place at the U.S. Open, but that fact doesn't tell the whole story. He stood at the 72nd hole with a great chance to win or get into a playoff, but he double-bogeyed the 18th hole to finish one shot back. He also finished in a tie for third at the 1999 PGA Championship. In the years to come, it seems the one thing left for the steady and reliable Cink to accomplish is the addition of a major title to his already impressive career. ■

There are few young golfers in the world who have done as much in the early years of their career and whose future looks as bright as does Luke Donald's. A star, both in Europe and the U.S., in stroke play and match play, he has as good a chance as any to some day wrest the number-one spot from Tiger Woods.

In 2006, for instance, he finished seventh on the money list in Europe and ninth on the PGA, a double success that is rarely achieved, both because of the fierceness of the competition and also the incredible endurance necessary to play such a hectic schedule on two continents. On the PGA Tour, Donald placed in the top 10 an amazing 10 times in just 18 tournaments and missed only two cuts. In Europe, he made more than $3 million to go with his $3 million in the U.S., making him one of the top worldwide money winners in '06.

Donald's 2006 PGA season was highlighted by a victory at the Honda Classic, a victory salted away under pressure. In the fairway at the 18th hole on Sunday, he held a one-shot lead over Geoff Ogilvy. Responding to the tense situation, he hit a perfect 5-iron from 199 yards to within four feet. He made

the birdie putt to win by two shots. A short time afterward, he tied for second at the Scottish Open and later tied for second at the Volvo Masters, another significant European event.

Then, in the 2006 PGA Championship, after 54 holes, Donald was tied with Tiger Woods, but he could manage only a 74 on the last day and finished third behind Woods, who won the event. Nonetheless, the result was Donald's best at a major tournament, and he was one of only 10 golfers to make the cut in all four majors in 2006.

As a kid, Donald was a prodigy. He was a serious golfer by his early teens, as was his brother, Christian. But where Donald continued to improve, Christian gave up serious golf and later became his brother's caddy, a tenure he continues to enjoy. Donald won the 1999 NCAA individual championship and turned pro in the summer of 2001. As a full rookie the next year, he won his first tournament, albeit thanks to a little luck. He was leading the Southern Farm Bureau Classic after 54 holes, but bad weather forced the cancellation of the final round on Sunday. When the weather didn't improve on Monday, the tournament was declared over and Donald the winner after just three rounds.

His double life started seriously in 2004. Donald won twice on the European Tour and had four top-10 finishes on the PGA Tour. The combined success earned him a spot on the Ryder Cup team for the International side which hammered the U.S. that year. He made the Ryder Cup team again in 2006 and was a perfect 3–0–0 in his matches, twice winning in the foursomes with Sergio Garcia and winning in the singles match on Sunday with a 2-and-1 decision over Chad Campbell.

Donald finished the 2004 season by teaming with Paul Casey to win the World Golf Championships-World Cup in Spain. More than anything, Donald disproves the merit of the many golf statistics that are now kept by the PGA. He is not a long hitter (ranked well over 100 in that stat), and isn't even among the most accurate off the tee. Yet, he has been among the very best in

CAREER *HIGHLIGHTS*

Turned Pro: 2001
PGA Wins: 2
First PGA Win: 2002
Best Season-end Placing: 9th (2006)
Ryder Cup: 2
Presidents Cup: n/a

scoring average for the last few years. Donald is a master putter with a terrific touch around the green, giving him the ability to save par on a rough hole and earn birdie off a great approach shot. He is not yet part of that elite group that includes Woods, Mickelson, Els, and Goosen — but he's not very far back, either. ■

TREVOR *IMMELMAN*

Born: Cape Town, South Africa, December 16, 1979

Most players talk the talk, but Immelman had to walk the walk. So often a player will say he'll withdraw from this major or that if his wife is ready to deliver a baby, and then it turns out she is able to hang in there until after the 72nd hole before delivering. Not Immelman, prior to the vaunted British Open in 2006. He had his tee time; he was in Royal Liverpool in England practicing; he got word his wife was about to deliver; he withdrew and flew back to Florida to be with her.

When he was five years old, little Trevor told his parents he wanted to be the best golfer in the world. These words carried special import for his father, Johan, who was commissioner of the Sunshine Tour in South Africa. By the time Trevor was 12, he was a scratch golfer and proving himself in junior tournaments across the country.

In the mid-to-late 1990s, Immelman was a force as a junior, and turned pro at 19, playing low-level tournaments in his home country before moving to the European Tour. He had made the cut as an amateur at the 1999 Masters after winning the USGA Public Links tournament the

previous year to qualify. In 2000, his second year as a pro, he won his first senior title, the 2000 Players Championship in South Africa. In 2002, he finished runner-up three times, and in 2003, he won the South African Open in extraordinary fashion. He and Tim Clark were tied after 72 holes, and on the first playoff hole Immelman took his 169-yard approach shot from the fairway and landed it within inches of the cup. He tapped in for the victory. Later that year, he teamed with countryman Rory Sabbatini to win the World Cup.

Immelman landed in the winner's circle twice in 2004, the first time in successful defense of his South African Open championship — the first time it had been done since Gary Player almost 30 years earlier. He then won the SAP Open TPC of Europe.

Although playing in Europe was important to Immelman, his real goal was the PGA. He played about a dozen tournaments between 2003 and 2005, making the majority of the cuts and getting his feet wet on the toughest tour of them all. Everything changed for him in 2005, though, when he was named to the Presidents Cup team. Not only was he part of that historic tournament, his participation automatically gave him two years' exempt status on the PGA Tour.

In 2005, Immelman finished in a tie for fifth at the Masters, and in 2006 he had a tremendous first full year on the PGA Tour. He won his first tournament, the Western Open, after a long birdie on the final hole gave him a two-stroke victory over Tiger Woods and Matt Goggin. Immelman had a series of superb finishes besides. To wit, a second-place finish at the Wachovia Championship after losing a playoff to Jim Furyk; a runner-up finish at the Byron Nelson Championship; and a fifth-place finish at the Canadian Open. In all, Immelman had eight top-10 finishes, earned nearly $4 million, and was named Rookie of the Year.

A year later, he had cooled his jets and missed several cuts. But after making some adjustments with swing coach David Leadbetter, he posted two third-place finishes early in the season and

the next year qualified for the 2007 Presidents Cup team. Immelman has been a pro for almost a decade, even though he is still a couple of years away from his 30th birthday. One of the bright lights in the world of golf, his is a name that will be on the leaderboard for many years to come, and he will win his fair share of events. Of that there can be no doubt. ■

CAREER *HIGHLIGHTS*

Turned Pro: 1999

PGA Wins: 1

First PGA Win: 2006

Best Season-end Placing: 7th (2006)

Ryder Cup: n/a

Presidents Cup: 2

JUSTIN *LEONARD*

Born: Dallas, Texas, June 15, 1972

As dour as any player on the gold circuit, Justin Leonard is bland and without much color. However, he has been a consistent performer since turning professional in 1994, and he has won one of golf's four majors, making him an instantly respected player on this merit alone.

Leonard's first Tour win came in 1996 at the Buick Open where he won by a comfortable five-stroke margin. But his career highlight came early on, at the 1997 British Open, played that year at Royal Troon. Leonard started the tournament with a 67 and followed with a 66 to move to within just two strokes of the lead. He was five back of Jesper Parnevik after 54 holes, but on the final day he shot a remarkable 65 to beat Parnevik and Darren Clarke by three strokes, giving him the claret jug that goes with the win, just after his 25th birthday.

Leonard won the Kemper Open earlier in 1997 and almost won the PGA Championship later in the year. These were among his many successes that season which placed him fifth overall on the money list, making him one of the apparent stars of the future.

Leonard hovered in lofty territory for several more years, winning at least once most years, but under-performing at the majors. He finished in eighth place at the 1998 Masters but has missed many cuts in the top tournaments and finished well away from the leaders most other times. Yet, on a week by week basis, he also never played too poorly, either.

The 1998 PGA Championship was another highlight victory for Leonard. Heading into the final round, he trailed leader Lee Janzen by five strokes, but he shot a 67 on Sunday to beat Tom Lehman and Glen Day by two shots. He came close to winning a second British Open in 1999. The tournament, made famous by Jean Van de Velde who held a three-stroke lead standing at the tee of the 72nd hole and collapsed with a triple bogey, featured a three-man playoff with Leonard, Van de Velde and Paul Lawrie, which Lawrie eventually won.

Without question, it was his performance at

CAREER *HIGHLIGHTS*

Turned Pro: 1994

PGA Wins: 10 (1 major)

First PGA Win: 1996

Best Season-end Placing: 5th (1997)

Ryder Cup: 2

Presidents Cup: 4

the 1999 Ryder Cup that has made his reputation as much as his British Open win, although that shining moment was marred by controversy. That year, the Europeans built a seemingly insurmountable lead over the U.S. through the first two days, but on the last day the Americans staged a remarkable comeback, crowned by Leonard. In his singles match against Jose Maria Olazabal, he found himself 4-down early on and looked to be out of it. But he won four straight holes to tie the match heading to the 17th hole, and it was there he sank a 45-foot putt to give the Americans victory. The controversy came when his teammates ran onto the green to celebrate, even though Olazabal still had a chance to tie the match, an extraordinary breach of sportsmanship in a sport founded on gentlemanly conduct.

Leonard had also played in the 1997 Ryder Cup as well as four Presidents Cups and two World Cup tournaments between 1996 and 2005. In 2005, he had a 3–1–1 record at the Presidents Cup.

Between 2000 and 2003, Leonard won one tournament every year while finishing runner-up five times in those four years. He played consistent if unspectacular golf, representative of his style of play. He is not a long hitter or a brilliant iron player, nor is he known for his skill around the green or for his putting. He simply does everything well.

In 2001, Leonard revamped his swing à la Tiger Woods. Although he adjusted very quickly, he has not enjoyed the same success in recent years as he had at the start of his career. Other young players have come up through the ranks and surpassed him, and his world ranking suffered badly in 2006 when he dipped to 106th on the money list. In 2007, he missed the cut in the first six tournaments he entered, his worst stretch play in his career. He rebounded in July to tie for second at the Buick Open, but his days of being in the hunt on Sunday of the major tournaments seem to be slipping away. ∎

Another of a small group of devout Christian players on tour, Steve Lowery has been on the course for a quarter of a century, and although he has won just two PGA tournaments, he has left his mark nonetheless with his perseverance and dedication.

Lowery turned pro in 1983 after a college career at the University of Alabama, but it took him fully four years before he got through Q-school to earn his PGA Tour card for the 1988 season. He made only half the cuts in 34 events, though, and as a result of finishing 157th on the money list, found himself right back playing in the Tournament Pro Series, the mini-tours which allow golfers to eke out a living and keep alive their dreams of one day playing on the PGA Tour. The demotion, as it were, lasted several years, but when he made his way back to the PGA he was a more mature golfer and ready for the challenge.

After a strong year on the Nationwide Tour in 1992, in which he had seven top-10 finishes, Lowery had a fine year on the PGA Tour in 1993, and the year after won his first tournament. That win, at the Sprint International under the Stableford system of scoring, was the result of two eagles on the back nine of the final round to get into a playoff with Rick Fehr. On the first extra hole, Lowery won with a par. Later in the year, he had a second-place finish (at the Buick Invitational) and a third-place result (at the World Series of Golf). By this time, he could well enjoy the satisfaction. A great college career had given way to nine separate trips to Q-school, but finally he could tell himself he had made it. He has never had to go back to Q-school since.

That victory at the International, however, was a blip on the screen more than a sign of things to come. Lowery became a consistent golfer, and his belief in Jesus kept him at an even keel through tough times. Those times included an

awful summer in 1999. After walking off the green at the end of the Tuscon Open, officials broke the news to him that his house in Orlando had burned to the ground. His family was safe, though, and he believed this was a sign to return home, to Birmingham. He did, and over the winter he dedicated himself to playing well the following year.

In 2000, Lowery delivered on those promises to himself. He had nine finishes in the top-10, including a win at the Southern Farm Bureau Classic. He birdied the 72nd hole of that event to force a playoff with Skip Kendall and then holed a 45-foot birdie putt from off the green on the first extra hole for the win.

Since then, Lowery has flirted with greater success. He finished in third place at the 2001 PGA Championship and had three second-place finishes the next year. In 2003, he led the B.C. Open after 54 holes, but Craig Stadler shot a final round 63 to win. The 2004 Western Open was more hard luck, as he led after 36 holes and finished in second place. At the 2006 FBR Open, he finished second, his ninth career runner-up finish.

Lowery had a poor 2007, leaving him vulnerable for the following year. He is still a couple of years away from joining the Champions Tour, so until then he will have to qualify and scramble for PGA Tour participation. Yet from 1993 to 2006,

Lowery finished lower than 92nd on the money list only once. Perhaps it was his belief in Christ that kept him going; perhaps it was his solid swing. More likely, it was a combination of the two, the spiritual happiness necessary for giving the golfer the confidence to play the game his way. ∎

CAREER *HIGHLIGHTS*

Turned Pro: 1983
PGA Wins: 2
First PGA Win: 1994
Best Season-end Placing: 12th (1994)
Ryder Cup: 0
Presidents Cup: 0

ROCCO *MEDIATE*

Born: Greensburg, Pennsylvania, December 17, 1962

The life and times of Rocco Mediate start and begin with his back, a part of his anatomy that has caused him ongoing pain during his golfing career. Indeed, his back has come to define his career, for better and worse. He was one of the first players to use a long putter, to relieve pressure on his back; and in 1991 he became the first PGA Tour player using the long

putter to win a tournament when he captured the Doral-Ryder Open. Appropriately, he won that tournament thanks to his putter. He birdied the final two holes to get into a playoff with Curtis Strange and then buried another birdie on the first extra hole to win.

Mediate was a late arrival to golf. His prime passion growing up was baseball, but by the time he got to Florida Southern College, he was intent on a career with sticks, not bats. He turned pro in 1985 but had a tough time in the early going. He had to go to Q-school in both '85 and '86, and although he earned his PGA Tour card both times, he made only a few cuts each year. It took him more than 140 tournaments to win for the first time, at Doral in 1991, and it took another two years before he got his second victory.

In 1993, Mediate made it to a playoff with Steve Elkington at the Kmart GGO event and birdied the fourth extra hole to win. Then the back troubles started. He missed more than two years with a ruptured disc, but when he returned it seemed, if anything, his game had improved. Mediate's 1996 season, which he started under special medical exemption, saw him make four top-10 appearances, notably a tie for fourth place at the Players Championship, a result achieved by making birdie the last six holes in succession.

This string of fine finishes in 1996 allowed him

CAREER *HIGHLIGHTS*

Turned Pro: 1985

PGA Wins: 5

First PGA Win: 1991

Best Season-end Placing: 15th (1991)

Ryder Cup: 0

Presidents Cup: 0

to regain his Tour card with all the privileges, but it wasn't until 1999 that he won again. Mediate claimed the Phoenix Open, earned nearly $1 million that year, and finished 37th on the money list. He won again in 2000 at the Buick Open, but his injury woes returned as a result of a freak accident. He was sitting in a chair on the patio prior to the PGA Championship when the chair gave way. Mediate fell, hit his head on a railing, hurt his shoulder and back, and was forced to withdraw after an opening round of 77.

Mediate won for the fifth, and perhaps last time, in 2002, at the Greater Greensboro Chrysler Classic. His back started to bother him again in 2003 and has never really let up. He has played since on various exemptions, but has had few results to be pleased with. In 2006, he made only eight of 18 cuts and finished a distant 206th on the money list.

The wear and tear on his body forced Mediate to consider a career change, and in 2007 he worked part-time as a course reporter for the Golf Channel. Ironically, he also had a fairly decent year as a player, making more cuts, earning bigger paydays, and enjoying the game more.

Since turning pro in 1985, Mediate seldom competed for a major championship. His first top 10 didn't come until 2001 when he finished fourth at the U.S. Open, but one of his better chances for winning came at the 2006 Masters. He was tied for fourth after three rounds, but his back hurt him on the final day, and he carded an 80 to finish 36th. That score included a dubious 10 at the par-3 12th, a hole that perhaps single-handedly took a green jacket away from him.

Despite the tough times and bad back, Mediate has won more than $13 million on tour and played in more than 500 PGA Tour events. He switched to the traditional putter in 2003, but his win back in 1991 with the belly putter gave many other pros the confidence to use what was then pioneering equipment. If he moves to reporting full-time, he can leave knowing that he has left his mark on the game, albeit a painful one. ∎

JESPER *PARNEVIK*

Born: Stockholm, Sweden, March 7, 1965

The three qualities about Jesper Parnevik that leap to the fore have nothing to do with his golf swing. One, he is the son of Bo Parnevik, a legendary comedian in Sweden on par with, say, Bob Hope or George Burns. Two, he wears clothing ranging from stylish to outlandish. Three, he and his wife had a nanny named Elin Nordegren. Elin who? Elin as in Mrs. Tiger Woods!

On the first score, perhaps, it's his father's career and success that has made Jesper such an extrovert. On the second, his friend Johan Lindberg designs all his clothes and gives him a refreshingly colorful appearance on tour. Lastly, after much prodding from Tiger, Parnevik finally

introduced the world number-one golfer to his nanny, and they hit it off sensationally.

Parnevik's golf career can be distilled to three heart-breaking finishes at the British Open, the tournament where he has finished in the top-10 six times in eleven appearances, by far his most consistent and impressive of the four major championships.

In 1993, in his first major, Parnevik finished a respectable 21st at the British Open. The next year, he had an exceptional chance to win. Standing at the tee of the 72nd and final hole, he held a two-shot lead on the field. He was so focused on the finishing hole that he forgot to look at the leaderboard. He made bogey on that final hole,

CAREER *HIGHLIGHTS*

Turned Pro: 1986

PGA Wins: 5

First PGA Win: 1998

Best Season-end Placing: 8th (2000)

Ryder Cup: 3

Presidents Cup: 0

and it cost him dearly. Nick Price eagled the 16th hole, birdied the 17th, and made par at the 18th to win the tournament by one stroke.

The next disappointment came at Troon three years later. Parnevik's 66 in the third round gave him a two-shot lead over Darren Clarke and put him five strokes up on Justin Leonard, but he closed with a 73 on Sunday and lost to Leonard. Typical of his play, he bogeyed the par-5 6th hole after gambling by going for the pin with his second shot.

The very next year, at Royal Birkdale in 1998, he again was the leader after 54 holes but, with weather playing in the players' favor on the final day, he was unable to close out the win, finishing fourth, two strokes back.

Perhaps as much as Phil Mickelson used to get all the attention for his risky tee shots and throw-caution-to-the-wind irons, Parnevik remains something of a renegade on the course. His shot management, as they say, has never been his strong suit, so much so that it might seem like he willfully takes himself out of contention through wild and erratic play.

Parnevik played in Europe for seven years (1986–93) before deciding to give the PGA Tour a try. He qualified through Q-school in 1993 and has played more frequently in the U.S. than Europe ever since. His first Tour win was the Phoenix Open in 1998, a result he celebrated by naming his firstborn Phoenix. Parnevik became only the second Swede ever to win on the PGA. He won again in 1999 (Greater Greensboro), 2000 (Bob Hope and Byron Nelson Classic), and 2001 (Honda Classic), but this four-year streak has been followed by a barren run ever since. Oddly, his best finish in a major on U.S. soil was a tie for fifth at the 1996 PGA Championship.

Parnevik has played in three Ryder Cups, most memorably in 1999 when he had a 3–1–1 record. He also played in 1997, when he had the distinction of being paired with countryman Per-Ulrik Johansson, winning the match against Jim Furyk and Tom Lehman 1-up. His colorful personality and matching wardrobe, featured in PGA commercials, have made Parnevik a welcome addition to the PGA Tour. ∎

KENNY *PERRY*

Born: Elizabethtown, Kentucky, August 10, 1960

If ever a golfer belonged in Oliver Sacks's book *Awakenings*, it would be Kenny Perry. A neurologist, Sacks worked with patients at a chronic-care hospital. He gave them a revolutionary drug, and for a brief time they "awoke" and led spectacularly normal lives, only to fall back into an inarticulate state after the drug was discontinued because of side effects.

Well, Perry's "awakening" occurred in the summer of 2003. By this time, he had been a pro golfer for 21 years and had won only four tournaments in that time. But at the height of the 2003 season, he won three times, finished second another time, made 24 cuts in 26 tournaments, won more than $4 million, and finished an exceptional sixth on the money list. After that, he won twice more in 2005 and that was it. He returned to a comparably benign state.

There was nothing to suggest Perry's 2003 dominance was about to happen. In the previous seven years, he had just one Tour victory to his credit. In 1996, he bogeyed the 72nd hole and went on to lose the PGA Championship to Mark Brooks on the first playoff hole. He had several top-10 finishes which got him onto the Presidents Cup team that year, but that was the last sniff of success he had prior to 2003.

His rejuvenation at age 42 started at the Bank of America Colonial tournament when he had the lead after three rounds, thanks to a course record 61 on Saturday. He breezed to a six-shot win. The very next week he won again, at Jack Nicklaus's Memorial Tournament, and followed this up by finishing in a tie for third at the U.S. Open. He had qualified to play that major only five times previously, and his best finish came at his first try in 1993, when he placed 25th. The next time out after the U.S. Open, Perry won again, this time at the Greater Milwaukee Open, again after leading through 54 holes.

CAREER *HIGHLIGHTS*

Turned Pro: 1982

PGA Wins: 9

First PGA Win: 1991

Best Season-end Placing: 6th (2003, 2005)

Ryder Cup: 1

Presidents Cup: 3

This incredible play earned Perry a spot on the U.S. team for the 2003 Presidents Cup, where he earned four of a possible five points. Just a year later, at the 2004 Ryder Cup, he played only twice, losing both matches. In 2005, he won just once and lost three times at the Presidents Cup.

In 2005, Perry had a mini-*Awakenings* season, winning two more tournaments. His win at the Bay Hill Invitational was impressive for its dramatic conclusion. Although he led after 36 and 54 holes, he arrived at the tee box on the 72nd hole in a tie with playing partner Vijay Singh. Singh put his approach shot in the water, though, and Perry made par for the win. Perry later won the Bank of America Colonial for the second time as well.

Perry is easily identified by his paunch, colorful shirts, and unorthodox swing. The paunch is nothing unique on tour, to be sure, but his backswing is one never to be taught at any school.

Instead of bringing the club back in a smooth, wide arc, it looks as though he takes the club from behind the ball and lifts it directly behind his ear before retracing his motion until impact. Yet for Perry, the swing works.

Perry is a proud Kentuckian who loves golf and gives a great deal back to his community. He helped design and build the only public course in his hometown of Franklin, and he has donated large sums to Lipscomb University in Nashville to help develop golfers.

Of course, Perry could never explain why, for a few months in 2003, he was the best golfer in the world — and he was. He did nothing different to what had made him a steady presence on the Tour for two decades, but for that brief time everything that was supposed to happen, did. What he planned, worked, and what he envisioned turned into reality. Never before and never since was he as dominant. ■

Into the genteel world of golf came Rory Sabbatini, quick-playing renegade. In a game defined by its sportsmanship and gentlemanly conduct, etiquette, tradition and respect for fellow golfers, Sabbatini made headlines around the world during the final round of the 2005 Booz Allen Classic by breaching protocol and flouting convention.

On that Sunday, he was paired with Ben Crane, a notoriously slow golfer who had frustrated Sabbatini all day with painstakingly deliberate shot-making. Indeed, the pair had been warned about slow play by officials earlier in the round (Crane later admitted the fault was all his). Sabbatini finally snapped on the 17th hole.

As the players approached the green, Crane's ball was furthest away and he was set to putt. But such was Sabbatini's frustration with his partner's slow play, that he walked right up to his ball, putted twice, and walked off before Crane could approach his own ball. It was a decided breach of decorum. Some players sided with Sabbatini because of Crane's play; others said that no matter what one's partner does, etiquette and civility must always be upheld.

Despite his indecorous behavior, Sabbatini is not unpopular. In fact, he has developed a following in the Rowdy Roadies: a group of fans who travel the world over to watch him play.

Sabbatini attended the University of Arizona on a golf scholarship and from there went directly to the PGA Tour in 1999 after qualifying through

CAREER *HIGHLIGHTS*

Turned Pro: 1998

PGA Wins: 4

First PGA Win: 2000

Best Season-end Placing: 4th (2007)

Ryder Cup: n/a

Presidents Cup: 1

Q-School. As a rookie, he made a solid impact, making half his cuts and finishing in the top 125 on the money list, a feat he has accomplished every year since. Sabbatini earned his first Tour win in 2000 at the Air Canada Championship. He capped a fierce comeback by making birdies at the 71st and 72nd hole of the tournament to win.

In 2003, Sabbatini had two major successes. First, he won the FBR Capitol Open, and later he and partner Trevor Immelman won the World Cup for South Africa, defeating the English tandem of Justin Rose and Paul Casey. The pair renewed their partnership two years later, but finished fourth.

Sabbatini elevated his game to the next level in 2006, when he earned nearly $3 million in official winnings and finished 12th on the money list. In all, he had five top-10 finishes, including a win at the Nissan Open. It was a tournament he almost let slip away. He had a four-shot lead at the start of the final round, only to fall back into a tie with Adam Scott. But on the 16th hole, Sabbatini put his tee shot on the short par 3 to within five feet. He made the birdie putt and came home in par-par fashion to win by that single shot.

Sabbatini's most recent victory was at the 2007 Colonial in a three-way playoff. He made birdie on the first extra hole, bettering Jim Furyk and Bernhard Langer for his fourth Tour win. All three finished 72 holes at –14, but Sabbatini drained his 15-foot putt for the win. It followed an impressive showing at the Masters where he finished tied for third, by far his best finish at a major. In fact,

before 2007, Sabbatini had made the cut in only nine of 21 major appearances. His previous top showing was a distant 26th at the 2006 British Open. He used that strong Masters showing to make 2007 his best year, finishing tied for third in his next two tournaments before Colonial and finishing in the top 10 on the money list for the first time in his career. ∎

STEVE *STRICKER*

Born: Edgerton, Wisconsin, February 23, 1967

"U p-and-down" is a golf term that describes a player making two great shots near the green, one shot from a bunker or fringe and another a putt to save a par. It is a term more applicable, in Steve Stricker's case, to describe his career which has seen him (a) ranked fourth in 1996; (b) play without his Tour card in 2004 and 2005; (c) play in the final pairing of the 2007 British Open on Sunday. Indeed, his is the very essence of an up-and-down career.

Life looked pretty good for Steve Stricker when

he turned pro in 1990. He had a fine college career at the University of Illinois and, after several events on the Nationwide Tour, won his PGA Tour card through Q-school at the end of the 1993 season. In just his second event in 1994, Stricker tied for second at the Northern Telecom Open, and in 1995 he finished 40th on the money list. So far, so good.

Stricker broke into the top 10 in 1996 by finishing in the top three on seven occasions. This included two victories — the first at the Kemper Open, the second at the Western Open, where he won by eight strokes. He also played on the Presidents Cup team and boasted a 5–0 record on the Dunhill Cup team. Stricker earned more than $1.3 million, good enough for fourth on the PGA money list.

The bottom started to fall out the very next year, though. Unable to build on his great 1996 season, he lost confidence in his swing and ended up 130th on the money list. He recovered with a strong 1998 season in which he finished tied for fifth at the U.S. Open and second in the PGA Championship. In 2001, he won the Match Play Championship, but after that he fell off the map entirely.

Things got so bad for him that even when he had to return to Q-school to regain his Tour card, he refused, declaring that his game and confidence were so poor he couldn't survive six rounds of golf.

CAREER *HIGHLIGHTS*

Turned Pro: 1990

PGA Wins: 4

First PGA Win: 1996

Best Season-end Placing: 2nd (2007)

Ryder Cup: 0

Presidents Cup: 2

Instead, he relied on exemptions from his wins and others granted him through letters and phone calls asking for same. Out of the abyss came — somewhere, somehow — a renewed version of his old self. He adjusted his swing and got some good results, and by 2006 he had earned his card back the hard way — solid shot-making.

In 2006, Stricker was named Comeback Player of the Year. He made 15 of 17 cuts, earned nearly $2 million in prize money, and had seven top-10 finishes. Although he was still without a victory in some 100-plus tournaments, he was playing well again.

The next year, he was able to do what he hadn't been able to do a decade earlier — build on good play. In 2007, he played like a new man, finishing fourth at the Sony Open in Hawaii to start the season and continuing to play great golf all year. He finished solo second at the Wachovia Championship in May and the AT&T National

at the start of July. He then headed to Carnoustie for the British Open where he had not played since 2002.

After solid rounds of 71 and 72, Stricker was the big story on Saturday when he equaled the course record with a stunning 64. That left him in second place at –6, three shots behind Sergio Garcia. The two made up the final pairing on Sunday, but Stricker's putter, which had been like a magic wand in round three, looked like a broken branch on the final day. He missed three critical putts inside four feet over the first nine holes, which might have put him in the lead, and he had to settle for a 74 and an eighth-place finish. Nonetheless, at 40, Stricker was finding his comfort zone on the course and qualified for the Presidents Cup team, his first international appearance in more than a decade. He capped his renaissance with a fine 3-2-0 record in the U.S.'s impressive win over the International side. ∎

DAVID *TOMS*

Born: Monroe, Louisiana, January 4, 1967

Quiet, unassuming and one of the all-time money leaders in PGA history, David Toms doesn't impress with his flair or his gallery — he just plays solid golf. Perhaps no better indicator of the kind of player he is can be found than at his only win in the majors, the 2001 PGA Championship.

Toms started that tournament with rounds of 66 and 65 and added another 65 on Saturday. The turning point came at the long par-3 15th hole when he carded a hole-in-one to retake the lead in that third round, a lead he never relinquished. He was paired with Phil Mickelson in the final round, and the two fought — shot for shot — the whole way. The decisive moment came at the final hole with Toms ahead by one shot. This was a long par 4 that had been reduced from par 5 by the Atlanta Athletic Club in Georgia. It was a hole that gave the long-hitting Mickelson a distinct advantage over the short-hitting Toms. Indeed, Mickelson was on the green in two, while Toms had a less-than-perfect lie in the fairway and a long way to go. He elected to lay up in front of water guarding the green. He landed his lob wedge to within 12 feet, though, and after Mickelson missed his birdie putt, Toms drained his putt for par to win.

That 2001 season was the best of Toms' career. In addition to this major triumph, he won two other tournaments (the Compaq Classic of New Orleans and the Michelob Championship), lost in a playoff at another event (The Tour Championship), and had nine top-10 finishes in all. He earned nearly $4 million and finished third on the money list.

Toms relied on consistent and smart play to win. Because he wasn't a long-ball hitter, he had to stay out of the rough to succeed. This meant being accurate off the tee, first and foremost. It also meant developing a fine short game and a reliable putter. His success started early. Even as a teen he was a scratch golfer, but after turning pro in 1989, he had his share of ups and downs.

It wasn't until 1996 that he played full-time on the PGA Tour and left the Nationwide Tour behind. Once he did, he learned how to win at the highest level and has yet to forget. His first Tour victory came in 1997, but it was at the 1998 Masters that he made his first real impression: Toms fired a final-round 64 at Augusta to finish in a tie for sixth. On the back nine, he carded a

62 | **GOLF** *NOW!*

record 29, which in itself included another record: six straight birdies (holes 12 to 17).

His career hit a major bump in the road near the end of the 2003 season when he had wrist surgery, but he fought back, slowly but surely, to recover his form. Earlier that year he had won the Wachovia Championship in gut-wrenching fashion. He had a five-shot lead after 54 holes and was playing sensational golf until he reached the 72nd green. He took four putts to hole out, but he had had enough of a lead to still win by two shots, a most awkward conclusion to a fine week of play.

Little known is his success in match play. Toms won the World Golf Match Play title in 2005 by demolishing Chris DiMarco 6-and-5 in the 36-hole final, and his overall record is a fine 20–6. He has had less success representing the U.S. at the Ryder Cup and Presidents Cup, but has been on the team every year since 2002. That first year, he beat Sergio Garcia in the singles match and finished with a 3–1–1 record. In 2007 he was the unsung hero, posting a 4-0-1 record and quietly leading his team to victory at the Presidents Cup in Montreal.

In all, Toms has won 12 times on the PGA Tour and finished in the top-10 another 76 times. He is sixth overall in career winnings, a remarkable fact given most fans would not name him as being among the top six players of all time. Yet his competitive spirit, cloaked behind a smile and gentlemanly conduct, have stood him in good stead for nearly 20 years of professional golf. ■

CAREER *HIGHLIGHTS*

Turned Pro: 1989
PGA Wins: 12 (1 major)
First PGA Win: 1997
Best Season-end Placing: 3rd (2001)
Ryder Cup: 3
Presidents Cup: 3

SCOTT VERPLANK

Born: Dallas, Texas, July 9, 1964

Few players had the start to a career that Scott Verplank had. In 1985, while still an amateur, the 20-year-old won the Western Open, one of the more prestigious Tour events. He became the first amateur to win on tour since Canada's Doug Sanders won the Canadian Open in 1956. In the succeeding 20 years and more, Verplank has proved to be an enduring presence on the PGA Tour, winning five times and competing internationally for his country as well.

Verplank graduated from Oklahoma State University in 1986 and turned pro right away. He struggled his first two years and had to keep his card through Q-school, but in 1988 he had a breakthrough season by winning the Buick Open. The next several years were marred by an elbow injury that twice required surgery and long rehabilitation stints. He returned to form in 1998 when he finished 18th on the money list and won

the individual title at the World Cup of Golf. He was named Comeback Player of the Year on the PGA Tour.

It wasn't until 2000 that he won again, a drought that had lasted a dozen years. At that year's Reno-Tahoe Open he rallied from five strokes down after 54 holes to tie Jean Van de Velde, and on the fourth playoff hole he bettered Van de Velde with a birdie to win. That win set up Verplank's best year, winning the 2001 Canadian Open and finishing 10th on the money list. He also finished second at the Byron Nelson Classic, losing to Robert Damron in a playoff.

It was in 2002 that Verplank made his first appearance for the U.S. at the Ryder Cup. Four years later, he was on the team again and made history by carding a hole-in-one in his match against Padraig Harrington, to become the first U.S. player to score an ace in Ryder Cup play.

Despite his consistency, Verplank has been equally inconsistent when it comes to major appearances. He did not qualify to play all four majors in a single year until 1999, and between 1985 and 2006, he played in 49 majors and made the cut only 28 times. His best major showings were two seventh-place finishes: the 2001 PGA Championship and the 2004 British Open.

Nevertheless, Verplank has held his card every year since 1997 when he had to re-qualify through Q-school. His persistence and durability were evident in 2007 when he won the Byron Nelson Championship, holding off Luke Donald by a single stroke. It was a win some 22 years removed from his first win, and it was inspired by the tournament's eponymous legend himself. Verplank had been good friends with the great Nelson (who died in 2006) and was the beneficiary of much advice from him. It was Verplank's 21st playing of that tournament. Donald was leading by three strokes with just six holes to play, but he faltered and Verplank reeled off five birdies in seven holes (5th through 11th) to rally for the win. Later in the year, he was the star at the 2007 Presidents Cup in Montreal, compiling a perfect 4-0-0 record for the victorious American side.

There is no magic to Verplank's game. He hits the ball accurately, but not long, and he is one of the better putters on tour. Most of all, he can handle the pressure and plays well regardless the situation. Given his abilities, it is surprising that he has won just five times on tour, but he has finished second 11 times and in the top 10 some 70 times. He might not always win, but he is frequently in the thick of things. ∎

CAREER *HIGHLIGHTS*

Turned Pro: 1986

PGA Wins: 5

First PGA Win: 1985

Best Season-end Placing: 10th (2001)

Ryder Cup: 2

Presidents Cup: 2

BIG *HITTERS*

3

The players who usually draw the biggest cheers from the tee box are the Big Hitters, the men who pull out their Big Berthas or similarly-sized drivers and look down the fairway, not for a safe spot in the middle, but far beyond to the green, trying to get the ball there with one mighty wallop. But the players who "drive for show" are not very often the ones who "putt for dough." Their entertaining 350-yard drives often give them more trouble than the distance is worth. Still, the Big Hitters are lovable and amazing for their power, and their popularity is an important part of the game's appeal.

Top (L-R): Corey Pavin, Rich Beem, Davis Love III, Bubba Watson
Bottom: John Daly

RICH *BEEM*

Born: Phoenix, Arizona, August 24, 1970

A free-wheeling, fun-loving, carefree player who is more like John Daly than Tiger Woods, Rich Beem has reached the highest of the highs and lived with long stretches of the lowest of the lows. However, even if he never plays another round of golf, or never makes another cut, he will always be able to say that he was the 2002 PGA champion, beating Tiger Woods by a single stroke, on a tension-filled Sunday at Hazeltine Golf Course.

Beem turned professional in 1994, but it was hardly a smooth ride to the fortunes of the PGA Tour. He was so down on his game by 1995 in fact, that he quit and sold cell phones and car stereos for a living. It wasn't until 1999, when he got back into the game seriously, that he made it to the PGA Tour through Q-school in December 1998.

At first, Beem had few expectations as a pro, but in his rookie season he performed surprisingly well. This included a win at the Kemper Open, which gained him a payday of $450,000. Previously, his best check had been for a mere $5,000 as winner of the less prestigious Conrad Hilton Open in New Mexico the year before. In all, he made more than $600,000 on tour and a book on his first season called *Bud, Sweat, & Tees: Rich Beem's Walk on the Wild Side of the PGA Tour* by Alan Shipnuck was published. It was a colorful and frank account of the life Beem had led with his caddy, explicitly detailing the parties and late nights.

While winning the 1999 Kemper was a highlight, his few days in Carnoustie at the British Open the same year was a low point. He was charged with driving under the influence and missed the cut, poor play on the course being overshadowed by his embarrassment off the course.

Beem barely hung on to his Tour card in 2000 and 2001, but rallied to have a magnificent year in '02. He won twice, had five top-10 finishes, won nearly $3 million, and finished seventh on the money list. Most important was winning the PGA Championship. He entered that tournament after having won The International the previous week. This event uses a point system rather than a shot system for scoring. Thus, he arrived at the PGA tournament brimming with confidence.

During the first two rounds, Beem found

himself in a tie for the lead. After 54 holes, he trailed Justin Leonard by three shots, and this duo made up the final pairing. Just ahead of them, Tiger Woods was making a sensational charge on the back nine. As Leonard fell apart, Beem came to the fore. He made a sensational birdie at the 16th hole, parred the 17th, and three-putted the 18th with a two-stroke lead to beat Tiger by a single shot.

Throughout that day, he had not only remained calm, but consistently played *his* game. That is, he used the driver when an iron might have been the smart and conservative play; he aimed for the flags and chased birdies instead of aiming for the middle of the green and taking a routine par during the pressure of the final round; he was cocky when he could have been safe. The result was a career-changing win, ensuring his exemption from many events for the next five years or more.

But Beem's attitude has caught up with him.

He has never matured as a golfer to parlay that major triumph into a serious golf game that could take him further. The PGA remains his last victory and, as his exemptions run out, he continues to miss cuts, finish low down the list and endanger his success in the long-term. In 22 career majors, he has missed 14 cuts. The nerve and verve he used to win that one big championship has yet to reward him regularly. ■

CAREER *HIGHLIGHTS*

Turned Pro: 1994

PGA Wins: 3 (1 major)

First PGA Win: 1999

Best Season-end Placing: 7th (2002)

Ryder Cup: 0

Presidents Cup: 0

FRED *COUPLES*

Born: Seattle, Washington, October 3, 1959

The back pains started in 1994 and didn't let up. By the time 2007 rolled around, Fred Couples was physically able to play in only a handful of events, but he did play in the Masters and made the cut for the 22nd straight time, one shy of Gary Player's all-time record. As he approaches the big five-o, Couples can look back on a long career studded with achievement, none bigger than the year 1992.

It wasn't long after turning pro in 1980 that Couples established himself as a PGA star. He had a smooth and reliable swing, and a demeanor suited to the ups and downs of the game. This combination helped him to play weekend golf with regularity. In fact, Couples never had to go to Q-school or qualify for the tour.

His longevity is most apparent when one considers that for his first tour win, at the Kemper Open in 1983, he won a five-man playoff that included Dr. Gil Morgan and Barry Jaeckel, two oldsters long gone from the PGA by 2007! Further, Couples won his second tournament the next year by beating Lee Trevino in a playoff. That win was at the Players Championship (considered the fifth major), and ushered in the "Couples Era" in golf. For the next decade and more, he was one of the top golfers in the world.

In the five-year period from 1990 to 1994, Couples won eight tournaments and more than $4 million in prize money. In 1991 and 1992, he was the PGA's Player of the Year. But it was the latter of those seasons that gave him his place in history, and in which he had his finest moments. He finished number one in earnings and finished first, second or third in 8 of 22 tournaments. Most significantly, he won the Masters, the only major of his career, by coming from behind on the final day to win by two strokes. The win came during an extraordinary streak that saw him win three times and finish second twice in a five-week span.

Couples teamed with Davis Love III to win four successive World Cup of Golf championships (1992–95). Unfortunately, it was also during this time that he started to experience back pains serious enough to affect his game. In 1994, he was

CAREER *HIGHLIGHTS*

Turned Pro: 1980

PGA Wins: 15 (1 major)

First PGA Win: 1983

Best Season-end Placing: 1st (1992)

Ryder Cup: 5

Presidents Cup: 4

off the course for three months, battling a tear in the outer layer of a disc in his lower back.

He seemed to make a full recovery — winning twice in Europe the next year and winning a second Players Championship in 1996. But in truth, all was not well. Couples wasn't swinging the club with his usual casual confidence, and he wasn't scoring well, either. After winning two more tournaments in 1998, he went into a tailspin. Psychologically, that might have started at the '98 Masters when he led the pack after each of the first three rounds and had to settle for second place. Then, when he started to have mediocre years, he decided to give in to his back rather than fight it.

In 2003, he hired coach Butch Harmon to reconstruct his swing. Harmon had worked with Tiger Woods, and later with Phil Mickelson, and had a great reputation for understanding the mechanics of the swing. The two worked for hours every day until Couples developed a shorter, more compact swing which reduced the pressure on his back. The result was a fine 2003 season in which he won one tournament and made 17 of 18 cuts.

Nonetheless, Couples still suffers from the lingering effects of his back. In his prime, he played about 25 tournaments a year, but as early as the mid-1990s he was down to about 17. Although he has won more than $20 million on tour and some 15 tournaments, he is getting through the final years of his career uncomfortably. Still, one of his greatest moments came in 2005 when he was selected to play on the Presidents Cup team for the U.S. In singles play on the Sunday, he defeated a shocked Vijay Singh 1-up with a long birdie putt on the 18th hole — one of the most spectacular wins by an American in that tournament's history. That speaks to the competitor in Couples, regardless of the back. ■

JOHN *DALY*

Born: Carmichael, California, April 28, 1966

Perhaps the most popular player in the world not named Tiger, John Daly is loved for his "Everyman" appearance and character, but the deeper, darker, and less appealing truth is that his is an immense waste of talent. Before he was 30 years old, he had won two major championships. Since that time he has frittered away money, talent and a noble place in golf history.

Daly is the very opposite of Tiger. Large, carefree and without any sort of work ethic, he meanders from tournament to tournament, unleashes long drives that go 75 yards off target while galleries roar approval, shoots two rounds in the high-70s to miss the cut, and drives his RV to the next event. He claims to have lost more than $50 million in gambling over the years; has battled alcoholism and four wives; and has taken a once-promising career and thrown it away. Anti-Tiger, indeed.

In the beginning, starting in 1987, Daly was a humble member of the Nationwide Tour. He was successful at Q-school in 1990 to earn his PGA Tour card for 1991, and made a stunning entrance into the golf elite: At Crooked Stick in Indiana, home of the 1991 PGA Championship, Daly shot a 69 and 67 to take the lead after 36 holes. Then, on the weekend, he was steady with a 69 and 71 to win the tournament by three strokes over Bruce Lietzke. He ended the year 17th on the money list and seemed destined for greatness because of his ability to launch massive drives off the tee and produce a delicate touch around and on the green.

But Daly won only twice in the next three years: first at the 1992 B.C. Open and then at

CAREER *HIGHLIGHTS*

Turned Pro: 1987

PGA Wins: 5 (2 majors)

First PGA Win: 1991

Best Season-end Placing: 17th (1991)

Ryder Cup: 0

Presidents Cup: 0

the BellSouth Classic two years later. His personal life took over his golf life, and his celebrity status altered from talk of long drives and carefree golf to talk about alcohol and smoking.

He had his last great moments in 1995 during the British Open at St. Andrews. Leading after 36 holes, Daly looked to be in good position, but a third-round 73 moved him down to fourth place. He recovered with a great 71 to lead by one shot in the clubhouse, but Constantino Rocca stunned the gallery by holing a 70-foot putt from the "Valley of Sin," that treacherous area in front of the green which usually produces three-putts, not playoffs. The putt tied Rocca with Daly and sent the pair to a four-hole playoff, which Daly won easily after Rocca triple-bogeyed the third extra hole.

Since then, Daly's career has been in almost-never-ending tatters. He has missed more cuts than he has played on weekends and has played not carefree golf, but wild and reckless golf. He has been suspended from the tour, disqualified,

and penalized himself countless strokes for breach of rules such as hitting the ball while it is still in motion. He will use his driver on holes where it is simply golf suicide to do so, knowing the roar of the fans will offset any triple bogey that will likely ensue.

By 2007, Daly was playing on borrowed time, and his exemptions had almost all run out, except those from his 2004 win at the Buick Invitational. He has finished out of the top 125 six times in the last 11 years. Daly's specialty these days is Skins games and special appearances, events where he can be himself — reckless, amiable, without worry — and still make oodles of money. The big belly and cigarettes and long drives that are part of his routine have long gone out of fashion when they are on display only on Thursdays and Fridays, and the waste of talent is both a shame and of his own doing. His epitaph might read, "I did it my way," but it might also read, "What might have been never had a chance." ∎

JASON *GORE*

Born: Van Nuys, California, May 17, 1974

There are three ways to play golf on the PGA Tour on a regular basis. The first is through special invitation and sponsors' exemption. The second is through Q-school, that grueling end-of-year, six-round tournament, which is physically and psychologically the toughest test for a young golfer. The third is by winning three successive tournaments on the Nationwide Tour, a feat so rare that it makes winning the lottery look easy.

Jason Gore made it through to the PGA Tour via the last and most improbable of these options, going from a ranking of 668 at the start of 2005 to 88 by season's end, and going from being an utterly anonymous big man to PGA cherub in the span of just a few breath-taking months of poetic golf.

Gore has the size of John Daly, but none of the personal afflictions, neuroses or controversies. Instead, he has the smile of that aforementioned lottery winner, and he takes in the cheers of the gallery knowing he represents Everyman: the guy who loves golf and hustles his game on the Nationwide Tour and one day — some day, somehow — winds up competing on the Sunday for the U.S. Open.

Prior to 2005, there was little to suggest Gore had the superstar in him. He earned his Tour card for 2001 the old-fashioned way — through

CAREER *HIGHLIGHTS*

Turned Pro: 1997

PGA Wins: 1

First PGA Win: 2005

Best Season-end Placing: 81st (2007)

Ryder Cup: 0

Presidents Cup: 0

Q-school — but he finished a distant 178th on the money list, failed to re-qualify and was back on the Nationwide Tour where he had started in 1997. In 2003, Gore again made it back to the PGA, and again he went right back down after making just 12 of 30 cuts and finishing 176th in money.

But then in 2005, he had a tremendous year. He qualified to play the U.S. Open for the first time since missing the cut in 1998, his only other appearance in a major. Gore produced rounds of 71 and 67 to share the lead after 36 holes at Pinehurst No. 2, one of the toughest courses in the world. After 54 holes, he was three shots behind leader Retief Goosen, and the two played as the final group on Sunday. By this time, his infectious enthusiasm had made him a fan favorite, but he exploded with an 84 in the final round. He lost the tournament, but he won countless friends and admirers for his casual, friendly demeanor and his obvious enthusiasm for the game.

Gore went back to the Nationwide Tour with renewed confidence and won three straight tournaments, earning himself a rare promotion to the PGA Tour. Four starts later, he was champion of the 84 Lumber Classic, a one-stroke winner over Carlos Franco. This marked the first time that a "three-in-three" Nationwide player won a PGA event in the same season. In fact, Gore almost completed his hat trick in 2002, winning two straight events on the Nationwide Tour but failing to win his next start.

In 2006, for the first time in his career, Gore didn't play a single event on the Nationwide Tour, but he barely survived the rigors of the PGA. He made only 14 of 29 cuts and finished 118th on the money list, just inside the magic number of 125 for automatic qualifying for the next year. This was accomplished with a great fall rally, as he made the cut in 8 of his final 10 tournaments and posted three top-10 placings. In 2007, he fared even worse, but continued to soldier on. He loves golf so much, he could never wipe the smile off his face, even if it means having to play on the Nationwide Tour again. ■

DAVIS *LOVE III*

Born: Charlotte, North Carolina, April 13, 1964

Golfers lead very isolated, private lives, so when personal news of a player reaches the public it is a rare chance for fans to see their hero in a light other than as a great putter or long driver.

David Love III is a family man as much as a golfer. He often goes to tournaments in a big camper. He longs for the day his son, Dru, can caddy for him, the way his brother Mark has. He owns and operates a stable because his wife loves horses. The measure of this man is his family.

Love's dad was a respected teacher of the game who taught the boy everything he knew about the game. Love thought that when he had to endure the horror of his father's death in a plane crash in 1988 that he had done his struggling, but he was wrong.

In 2003, another personal tragedy offset Love's triumph of a career year with the clubs. He had hired his wife's sister's husband, Jeff Knight, to look after the family's personal finances, a role that expanded to include much more. What Love didn't know was that Knight was stealing large sums from the golfer while in his confidence. The subterfuge was discovered by the FBI, and although Love was prepared to help Knight deal with the charges and the ramifications, Knight committed suicide the day he was supposed to go to trial.

In 2003, Love won four tournaments by about the halfway point of the season. He started the year with a win at the AT&T Pebble Beach National Pro-Am, finishing with a birdie on the 72nd hole. He followed with a second-place finish at the Honda Classic and won the coveted Players Championship for the second time with a stunning 64 in the final round, turning a two-shot deficit into an easy six-stroke win. Most stunning was his win at the MCI Heritage Classic, his fifth career win at that tournament. He holed a long chip from the fringe at the final hole to force a

playoff with Woody Austin and birdied the fourth playoff hole to win that showdown.

At The International, he led from start to finish for his fourth win of the year and 18th of his career. And then, the Knight tragedy put a stop to his great year and his ebullient play on course. Although he finished third on the money

CAREER *HIGHLIGHTS*

Turned Pro: 1985

PGA Wins: 19 (1 major)

First PGA Win: 1987

Best Season-end Placing: 2nd (1992)

Ryder Cup: 6

Presidents Cup: 6

list and won more than $6 million, his emotional makeup was not what a golfer needs. In some ways, he has never fully recovered. Love has won only once since then — the 2006 Chrysler Classic — but despite his drought on course he has remained one of the most consistent golfers over the last 20 years.

The greatest criticism of Love's play has been his inability to play gritty golf, to dig deep and gut out a win, to play to beat his opponents. He is perhaps best known on course for his friendship with Fred Couples, a relationship that has had excellent results for the pair in championship play. The two were virtually unbeatable at the World Cup of Golf in the early 1990s, winning the marquee team event in 1992, 1993, 1994 and 1995. His record in Ryder Cup and Presidents Cup play, although solid, has not been spectacular.

Love was anything but a child prodigy, but his determination as a teen led him to the University of North Carolina where he improved by leaps and bounds. Always one of the longer hitters on tour, he has won one major, the 1997 PGA Championship at Winged Foot. He did it in style, claiming first prize with a five-shot win over Justin Leonard. He has also endured several injuries and has admitted that he let the problems linger, psychologically, lacking the fortitude to fight through or recover quickly in order to return to the Tour.

Love has earned colossal sums of money on the Tour and through endorsements, but with his superb ball striking ability, it leaves one wondering why he has not won more majors or been more of a force down the stretch of more tournaments. The talent is there. ∎

COREY *PAVIN*

After being a pro golfer for a quarter of a century, a few things are bound to change. For instance, the young Corey Pavin had a full head of hair under his golf cap and a nice, thick moustache between lip and nose. The Pavin of the 21st century shaves his head right down to the wood and has no facial hair to speak of. The early Pavin was also the top money maker in the world for a year, but the later incarnation has had more difficulty competing against a new generation of ball strikers.

Pavin turned pro in 1982, immediately after graduating from UCLA, and it took him just two years to earn his PGA Tour card to qualify for full-time play. In his first five years, he won seven tournaments, starting with the Houston Open in 1984. He had a career-defining season in 1991, leading the PGA in earnings with $979,430. This marked the last time the top PGA player earned less than $1 million. (By comparison, Vijay Singh led the Tour in 2004 with earnings just under $11 million.)

Pavin won twice in 1991 and had ten top-10 finishes. That year also marked the start of his resurgence, and over the next six years he won another seven tournaments and only once finished outside the top eight in earnings (in 1993, when he finished in 18th spot). Pavin finished second at the PGA Championship in 1994 and the next year captured his one and only major tournament to date, the U.S. Open.

The 1995 Open at Shinnecock Hills ended in remarkable fashion. Greg Norman led Pavin and the field by three strokes at the start of the final round, but as Norman did so often, he choked badly under pressure and gave the tournament away. Pavin played his way into contention and was in control in the 72nd fairway. He needed a par to win, but he was 228 yards away from the pin for his second shot at the par 4 finishing hole. He calmly hammered a 4-wood to within five feet of the flag, and although he missed the birdie putt, he tapped in for the one-stroke win over Norman.

Pavin won the Colonial Tournament the next

CAREER *HIGHLIGHTS*

Turned Pro: 1982
PGA Wins: 15 (1 major)
First PGA Win: 1984
Best Season-end Placing: 1st (1991)
Ryder Cup: 3
Presidents Cup: 2

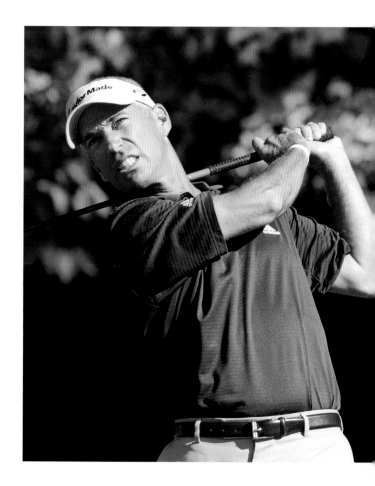

year and then inexplicably fell off the chart. He lost that consistency which had made him so successful, and his world rankings went into a free fall. He failed to win for a decade and more and was no longer a threat among his peers. Between 1997 and 2007, he played in 25 majors and missed the cut 14 times. In 2004 and 2005, he qualified only for the U.S. Open.

Yet Pavin persevered, and he came back in stunning fashion in 2006, albeit briefly. He won the U.S. Bank Championship by a two-stroke margin over Jerry Kelly. It was a win that began on the opening day when Pavin shot a 61, a career low. The round included a PGA Tour record 26 for the front nine as he birdied the first six holes in a row. His two-round total of 125 also tied the PGA record for low 36-hole score, but that amazing performance at Brown Deer Park Golf Course did not signal a long-term renaissance. This was his only top-10 finish of the year, and 2007 provided even more misery. Pavin missed the cut in nine of the first 14 tournaments he played and finished outside the top 125 for the sixth time in the last 11 years.

Since he won't qualify for the Champions Tour until late in the 2009 season, Pavin must continue to work through his struggles on the PGA Tour. He proved in 2006 that even after a long stretch of winless golf he still can play with the best on any weekend — but he has to find a way to do so consistently, or else he will find himself crawling to the Champions Tour instead of running to it. The former number-one earner in the world knows the proverbial sweet smell of success, but he has also swallowed the bitter pill of defeat only too often in the last decade. ∎

Not everyone can play golf like Tiger Woods, but even fewer golfers can dress like Duffy Waldorf. Not exactly built like Tiger either, Waldorf covers his ample load with colors that are the envy of a good paint store. His taste matches his personality, which is carefree and relaxed rather than pressure-filled and tense.

Waldorf turned pro in 1985 and, although he has won only four times on tour, he has played at a consistently high level for long enough to earn nearly $12 million on the golf course.

Waldorf's first PGA Tour win came at the La Cantera Texas Open in 1995 and was accomplished in impressive fashion. He led the field by just a single stroke after 54 holes, but his final-round 65 gave him a 6-shot win over Justin Leonard and a 12-shot win over the rest of the field. In 1992 he had been runner-up twice, and in 1994 he placed in the top 10 no fewer than eight times. After turning pro in 1985, Waldorf had a tough time of it. He went through Q-school four times, each time earning his card, each time finishing out of the top 125 and having to do it all again the next year.

His best year was 1999, when he won two tournaments and finished 28th on the money list. The first win that season came at the Buick Classic, a win he accomplished with gutsy shot-making in the clutch. He was co-leader after 54 holes, but trailed after 16 on Sunday. Waldorf

promptly birdied the 17th and 18th holes to force a playoff with Dennis Paulson. He then birdied the first extra hole to claim the victory.

He produced similar dramatics to win his second tournament of 1999 at the Texas Open,

CAREER *HIGHLIGHTS*

Turned Pro: 1985

PGA Wins: 4

First PGA Win: 1995

Best Season-end Placing: 23rd (1992)

Ryder Cup: 0

Presidents Cup: 0

the site of his other previous Tour win in 1995. Waldorf started the final round two shots off the leader (Stephen Ames), and after 72 holes he and Ted Tryba were tied and went to a playoff. Waldorf made a 45-foot putt for birdie on the first extra hole to win. The experience needed to win that playoff was partly attained in his appearance in the 1997 Michelob Championship. After leading by three shots heading into the final round, Waldorf ended up in a tie with David Duval and Grant Waite, only to lose on the first extra hole as Duval birdied to relegate Waldorf and Waite to second place.

His most recent win was, in many ways, his most impressive. It came in 2000 at the Golf Classic. Tiger Woods and Steve Flesch were six strokes clear of Waldorf, who was in second place after 54 holes, but Waldorf shot a 62 on the final day to win. His round included 10 birdies, the most important being a lengthy putt on the 18th which he drained with confidence. Not only did

he beat Tiger on Sunday, Waldorf accomplished this task during a year in which Tiger was all but unbeatable, recording nine wins.

Since 2005, Waldorf has been running on exemptions and qualifying to play most of his PGA Tour events. He has finished out of the top 125 each of these three years (2005, 2006, 2007), but he soldiers on. Perhaps as much as his clothing, he is known for his knowledge and love of wine. He'll happily go against the grain by suggesting many white wines are superior to reds, and his 1,800-bottle cellar attests to the seriousness with which he drinks and collects. Of course, no lover of wine is a complete person without a commensurate love of food, and Waldorf can match dish with drink with the best of them on the PGA. He's made a good living playing golf, and he's made a better life off the course because of it — a man who takes golf seriously and life casually. Is there a better combination? ∎

BUBBA *WATSON*

Born: Bagdad, Florida, November 5, 1978

Just as Wayne Gretzky had his backyard rink, Bubba Watson had his backyard golf course. He lived on a big piece of property which featured a dirt driveway, so he drew a five-foot circle and made this his one-hole golf layout.

Using a waffle ball, Watson would play shots over and around trees and other obstacles, learning how to "shape" his shots and use his imagination to get the ball to his drawn-up hole-in-the-driveway. Like Gretzky, Watson practiced his game all day every day, year after year. Truly a self-taught golfer, the only instructor he ever had was his father, who was a duffer at best. Nonetheless, Bubba made it to Faulkner State Community College and then to the University of Alabama where he established himself as the longest hitter around.

And, just as Eldrick Woods has been called Tiger since whenever, Gerry Watson has been called Bubba ever since his dad called him that as a newborn. Combine this nickname with his Elvis-style sideburns, and this is one unique golfer, to be sure.

A lefty — another oddity! — Watson has ranked first in driving wherever he has played. His pink-shafted driver currently carries the ball some 320 yards on average, tops on the PGA Tour. He had one start on the Nationwide Tour in 2001 and one on the PGA Tour the next year before settling in to a pro career in the former for all of 2003. Over the next three years, Watson made steady and continual progress, earning his full-time PGA Tour card for 2006.

Although he never won a tournament on the Nationwide Tour, Watson moved up the standings on the money list each year, from 63rd in 2003 to 37th in '04 and 21st in '05. Normally, only the top-20 moneymakers on the Nationwide Tour earn their PGA card for the next year, but Watson caught a break in 2005. That year, Jason Gore earned promotion during the season, thanks to three successive wins, so the Nationwide extended eligibility to the top 21 and Watson qualified that way.

Watson's rookie season on the PGA Tour in 2006 had plenty of confidence-building signs. His first start came at the Tour's season opener, the Sony Open in Hawaii, and he finished in fourth place, taking home a check for $244,800, more than he had ever won in any one *year*! More impressive, while the talk with Watson was always about the big club, he holed 67 of 70 putts inside 10 feet that week. "Drive for show — putt for dough," as they say. And he did.

In all, Watson had three top-10 finishes, earned more than $1 million, and finished a very respectable 90th on the money list in 2006. He also led the Tour in driving distance, averaging a mammoth 319.6 yards per drive off the tee. In 2007, he produced inconsistent, but sometimes brilliant, golf. In his first 17 tournaments, he played on the weekend only nine times, but five of those events saw him finish in the top 10.

Watson has left his career in the lap of the gods. He adamantly promises that the day he thinks he needs a golf lesson is the day he quits. He is part Phil Mickelson (early vintage), and part John Daly (for his abandoning of all reason, hitting whatever shot he wants without a sense of strategy or course management). Watson shuns planning and practicing, exercise and weight training and proper diet. He just goes out there and hits the ball, finds it and hits it again. That's not much of a philosophy, but so far it has stood him in good stead. Five years from now, he may be ranked in the top 10 in the world. Or, he may be back in Bagdad, Florida, whence he came, golfing with the good ol' boys. ■

CAREER *HIGHLIGHTS*

Turned Pro: 2001

PGA Wins: 0

First PGA Win: 0

Best Season-end Placing: 37th (2007)

Ryder Cup: 0

Presidents Cup: 0

YOUNG GUNS
& ROOKIES

4

The Young Guns of the Tour may, at present, lack consistency and that special nerve under pressure, but they are skilled, ambitious, and fearless in their quest for success. The Cream of the Crop and Tour Veterans must constantly reassert themselves and prove that they are the most dominant golfers in the game. They are being pushed all the time by the Young Guns, who are ready and willing to usurp the top players from their high rank. Although they may not win very often, and they may blow a tournament in the closing holes with regularity, they are nonetheless on a steep learning curve and are close to becoming top stars in the game.

Top (L-R): Camilo Villegas, Tadd Fujikawa, Adam Scott, Zach Johnson
Bottom: Sergio Garcia

CHAD *CAMPBELL*

Born: Andrews, Texas, May 31, 1974

With any luck, "the Chad" will be able to look back at his miserable 2007 season and see this *annus horribilis* as a blip in a surging and promising career, for the year was so much worse than anything he had experienced previously.

In fact, Campbell has been spoiled by his own success. He had a fine college career at the University of Nevada, Las Vegas, and after turning pro in 1996, he enjoyed success at every ever-greater level of play. Campbell started out on the Hooters Tour in 1997 and was named Rookie of the Year. He then led that tour in earnings in each of the next three years; was named Player of the Year in each of those years and, after 13 wins in that span, earned himself a place on the next rung up — the Nationwide Tour.

Campbell wasted little time in saying goodbye to that next level. In 2001, he was named Player of the Year on the Nationwide Tour, and earned his PGA card by virtue of winning three tournaments in one year. He joined the PGA Tour, and, in just his sixth start ever, finished second at the Southern Farm Bureau Classic.

As a full-time rookie in 2002, Campbell adjusted quickly to the world's top level of golf. He played a strenuous 34 tournaments and made 21 cuts, ensuring a place in the top 125 so he wouldn't have to go to Q-school (he finished 81st). In 2003, he established himself among the best young golfers around. He missed only two cuts all year and finished in the top 10 an incredible 13 times. But his crowning glory came at the end of the year when he beat the best of the best in the Tour Championship, the first player ever to make this event his first career victory.

Starting the tournament with solid rounds of 70 and 69, Campbell blew the door open with a 61 on Saturday to grab the lead by one shot. Campbell was relentless on the final day, finishing with a 68

and a three-stroke victory over Charles Howell III. This came just weeks after Campbell almost won his first major, the PGA Championship. He was one shot back of Shaun Micheel with one hole to play, but Micheel made a historic approach shot to the 18th and tapped in the birdie for the win. Campbell, meanwhile, earned nearly $4 million in 2003, good for seventh position on the money list. Not bad for a second career season on the PGA Tour.

Campbell continued to be a consistent top-10 golfer, a true sign that victory was always within reach. In fact, he was a genuine threat week in,

week out. He won for the second time early in 2004, coming from four strokes behind on the final day to win by six strokes over Stuart Appleby at the Bay Hill Invitational. His strong overall play earned him a place on the Ryder Cup team. He lost two matches in the pairings, but on the final day, Campbell handed Luke Donald a 5-and-3 loss, an impressive win, indeed.

Campbell finished runner-up twice in 2005 and won for the third time in '06, taking the five-day, 90-hole Bob Hope Classic by three shots over Jesper Parnevik and Scott Verplank. He later defeated Tiger Woods in the Match Play Championship and earned his second berth on the Ryder Cup where he went winless (0–1–2).

The world came crashing in on Campbell in 2007, though. He lost his confidence sometime after a strong performance in the Match Play Championship in February. Between March and August, he missed seven cuts in 13 tournaments, notably going home early at the Masters (where he had tied for third in 2006), the Players Championship, and the British Open. He also finished a distant 57th at the U.S. Open, a tournament in which he has made the cut only twice in eight career tries.

Campbell is too good not to bounce back from this dismal season, but on the PGA Tour nothing is given a player. If he bounces back, he'll have to do it on his own and, if he has learned anything, he knows bouncing back sooner is a lot easier and more tenable than bouncing back later. Sometimes later never comes. ■

CAREER *HIGHLIGHTS*

Turned Pro: 1996

PGA Wins: 4

First PGA Win: 2003

Best Season-end Placing: 7th (2003)

Ryder Cup: 2

Presidents Cup: 0

MICHAEL CAMPBELL

Born: Hawera, New Zealand, February 23, 1969

If Michael Campbell never wins another golf tournament, his place in the game's history is solidified. In 2005, he won the U.S. Open at Pinehurst No. 2, the first Maori to win the event and the first New Zealander to win a major since Bob Charles bettered the field at the 1963 British Open. Such was the importance of that win that the New Zealand Parliament delayed the day's proceedings to watch the final holes at Pinehurst.

Campbell grew up in the tiny area of Titahi Bay. He is of the Ngati Ruanui and Nga Rauru tribes, and his Maori heritage is an important part of his makeup. He was an athletic kid and got interested in golf by caddying for his dad at the local course. He started to play at age 10 and quickly became a superb golfer. At 16, he broke the Titahi course record and by 18 he was traveling the world representing New Zealand at

the top amateur tournaments. In 1992, he became the first New Zealander to win the Australian amateur championship.

Campbell turned professional the following year and devoted all his time and energy to golf. He won the Canon Challenge in just his fifth career start, a tournament on the Australasian Tour, and the next year he earned his European Tour card. His coming-out party on the world stage came at the 1995 British Open where he led the field after three rounds. Although he shot a final-round 76 to finish in a tie for third place, he now had the confidence to play with the world's best.

Unfortunately, that confidence suffered badly after a wrist injury that took him nearly two years to fully recover from, physically and psychologically. That recovery came during a brilliant performance at the Johnnie Walker Classic in Taiwan at the end of 1999. He beat a field that included Tiger Woods, Ernie Els and Geoff Ogilvy. That paved the way for 2000 when he won five events worldwide. His world ranking soared to 14th, and this status allowed him to play more events on the PGA Tour.

In the United States, however, Campbell struggled. In 2003, he entered 14 tournaments but made the cut only five times and earned only a little more than $100,000. In 2004, focusing more on Europe and Australasia, he was again a consistent and impressive performer and, as luck would have it, history and his life were about to change. The U.S. Open, known for its "open" status which allows absolutely anyone in the world the opportunity to qualify to play, introduced an "international qualifier" component to its structure. Campbell won a place for the 2005 U.S. Open and went to Pinehurst with enthusiasm but few expectations.

Campbell's first three rounds of 71, 69 and 71 had him just four strokes behind leader Retief Goosen. Then on Sunday, a day when over par was the average, he shot a 69 to hold off a surging Tiger Woods to win his first major and earn his place in New Zealand sports history. But he wasn't done there. He also finished fifth at the British Open and sixth at the PGA Championship. At

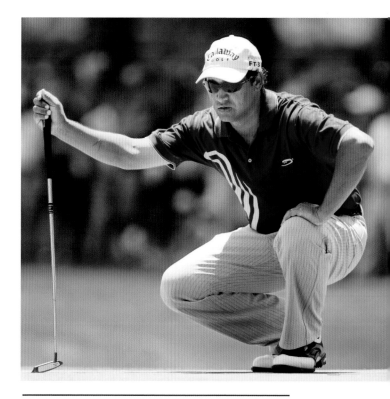

CAREER *HIGHLIGHTS*

Turned Pro: 1993

PGA Wins: 1 (1 major)

First PGA Win: 2005

Best Season-end Placing: 135th (1995)

Ryder Cup: 0

Presidents Cup: 2

the HSBC World Match Play Championship, he beat Goosen in the semifinals and Paul McGinley 2-and-1 in the finals to earn another significant victory. In all, 2005 was a career year for him.

Life on the PGA and around the world hasn't been so kind to Campbell since. In 2006, he missed the cut at the U.S. Open as defending champion, and he went winless worldwide. In 2007, he made less than $40,000 on the PGA Tour and struggled in Europe as well. Nonetheless, a man with Campbell's swing and competitive fire will no doubt find his form again and represent tiny New Zealand successfully in tournaments around the world. ■

TADD *FUJIKAWA*

Born: Honolulu, Hawaii, January 8, 1991

There is, quite simply, no better or more compelling story in golf than the life and golfing times of tiny Tadd Fujikawa, who made his way too soon into this world, but who has become a sensational golfer all the same.

Born three and a half months prematurely, Fujikawa weighed one pound, 15 ounces when he first breathed air outside the womb. Doctors gave him a 50-50 chance of surviving, and there was real danger that he could suffer from various defects or illnesses resulting from his tininess. But Tadd was a fighter, and although he grew up to be just 5'1", he had a love and passion for golf that has given him plenty more reason to live.

Few had heard of Fujikawa until the early summer of 2006 when he qualified for the U.S. Open. At age 15, he became the youngest qualifier since 1941, and he promptly went out and shot 81–77 to miss the cut. He disappeared and was forgotten until the Sony Open in Hawaii in January 2007 at the Waialae Country Club in Oahu.

There were two Hawaiians in that tournament. The first was Michelle Wie, the tall teenage sensation of women's golf who was given a sponsor's exemption. The second was Fujikawa, who earned his way into the event by winning the only amateur spot available through the Aloha section of PGA qualifying. Wie played badly over two days and missed the cut by 14 shots.

Fujikawa made the cut, becoming the second youngest player ever to do so (Fifteen-year-old Canadian Bob Panasik qualified for weekend play at the 1957 Canadian Open). Fujikawa avoided being cut by making a birdie at the 16th hole to get one shot inside the cut line. And then, as if to make clear this was no fluke, he eagled the 18th hole to earn his weekend rights emphatically.

Fujikawa didn't just scrape by, however. He birdied six of ten holes during one stretch of the

CAREER *HIGHLIGHTS*

Turned Pro: 2007

PGA Wins: 0

First PGA Win: 0

Best Season-end Placing: n/a

Ryder Cup: n/a

Presidents Cup: 0

third round to score a 66 and move up to eighth place. On Sunday, his round was accented by a 50-foot birdie putt, and a more normal round of 72 left him tied for 20th in the field, just nine shots behind the winner, Paul Goydos.

While Wie was making millions of dollars and not playing well, Fujikawa was attending Maunalua High School and being driven by his mom to the local golf course to learn the game on his own every night until dark. His mother Lori does clerical work at a car repair shop and dad Derrick is project manager for a local contractor. They leave the golfing to Tadd.

Just a month after his sensational showing at the Sony Open, Fujikawa won the Hawaii Pearl Open, becoming the first amateur to do so in 15 years. In the summer of 2007, he turned pro, a decision that had support and criticism both. On the one hand, he came from a family unable to afford the necessary coaching and support to get him to the top. On the other, he was still young enough and had many years ahead of him to play anonymously until going to college on a scholarship. Whether it works out, only time will tell, but one thing is certain: everyone who loves golf is rooting for tiny Tadd Fujikawa to succeed. ∎

SERGIO *GARCIA*

Born: Castellon, Spain, January 9, 1980

Considered to be the world's best golfer under 30, or the world's best golfer not to have won a major championship, Sergio Garcia will have to live a long time with the events of Black Sunday — July 22, 2007. That day, the final round of the British Open at Carnoustie, saw him experience the best day of his life, then the worst, then the best, and, finally, the worst. Only time will tell if he can recover psychologically from losing on a day in which he started as a three-shot leader on the field.

In fact, after a birdie on the eighth hole on Sunday, Garcia was leading by four strokes and looked to be the sure winner of the 136th British Open Championship. Then, everything unraveled. He made a string of bogeys; unheralded Argentine Andres Romero made a spectacular charge; and Padraig Harrington was quietly putting together the best round of the day by those in contention. Romero collapsed, and incredibly, Harrington had a one-shot lead at the 18th tee and gave it up to Sergio by the time he putted out (he put the ball in the water not once but twice). Garcia had a second life. He now stood at the 18th tee with a one-stroke lead. Par would give him his first career major.

Par was not to be. His approach shot found the bunker, and he took a bogey to force a four-hole playoff with Harrington. On the first extra hole, Harrington made a brilliant birdie, and another bunker gave Sergio another bogey. Harrington won by one shot, and Garcia was left crushed and emotionally damaged. He should have won, plain and simple.

Before turning pro on April 21, 1999, Garcia set numerous records under the rubric of "youngest to," notably to qualify for a European Tour event (at age 14) and to win, namely the European Amateur Championship (at age 15). As a rookie, he continued to be "youngest to" on the PGA Tour, notably to lead the PGA Championship.

But the single moment that catapulted him into the hearts of fans and his status into the best Tiger-challenger around came during the later stages of that PGA Championship. Standing on the 16th tee, he trailed Tiger by two strokes when his drive landed behind a tree. Eyes closed, he hammered a shot that flew up a hill and out of sight. Garcia ran up the fairway, leaping in the air to see where it had landed. The enthusiasm, the controlled recklessness of the shot, the challenge to Tiger, all endeared him to the gallery, and in that moment, Garcia the Spaniard became, simply, Sergio.

He finished one shot behind Tiger that day, and later in the year he became the youngest player in Ryder Cup history. Despite playing only eight PGA events, he finished 53rd on the money list. Garcia also won twice in Europe to solidify his place among the best young golfers in the world.

From those glorious moments, however, has sprung only intermittent greatness and many more moments of frustration and disappointment. Garcia has won six PGA events and 10 more in Europe, and he is certainly a formidable talent. But despite being one of the longest, strongest hitters on tour, he also suffers from a wonky putter that has caused him more heartache than 350-yard drive glory.

Garcia's oh-so-close play at Carnoustie in the 2007 British Open was the last in a long line of near misses that include a second-place finish at the Players Championship earlier in 2007, a tie for third at the PGA Championship in 2006, a tie for third at the 2005 U.S. Open and a tie for fourth at the 2004 Masters. Are these scores signs of someone unable to close out a pressure situation with a win, or are they signs that one of these days he'll settle into a comfort zone coming down the stretch of a major?

Only time will tell, but after 2007, Sergio is going to have to calm his nerves, not in the clubhouse or in some weekly Tour event, but on the 18th tee box of a major championship that he's leading by one shot on a Sunday. ∎

CAREER *HIGHLIGHTS*

Turned Pro: 1999

PGA Wins: 6

First PGA Win: 2001

Best Season-end Placing: 6th (2001)

Ryder Cup: 4

Presidents Cup: 0

There are so many world-class golfers on various tours across the globe it's intimidating. Yet Todd Hamilton, an itinerant ball striker if ever there was one, proved that even for one week he could be Tiger Woods. His 2004 season was so extraordinary for this otherwise journeyman player that one marvels at why he hasn't won more often or why he won at all. But history will always show that Todd Hamilton was the 2004 British Open champion.

Although Hamilton turned pro in 1987, he played almost all of the first 16 years of his life far away from the glamour and riches of the PGA Tour. Most every year he tried to qualify through Q-school, and after each failed attempt he went to the Far East and played on the Asian Tour where he was a star. In 1992, frustrated and despondent by his lack of success at home, he almost packed it in. But he talked himself out of it and went on to win three tournaments while leading the Asian Tour in money winnings for the season, earning himself his pro card on the superior Japan Tour. It was there he played for the next 10 years.

A typical season had Hamilton play a few events in Japan, come to the U.S. for one tournament and some rest, and then go back to Japan. At year's end, he would try for his PGA Tour card, fail, and repeat the cycle all over again. Yet, for whatever

CAREER *HIGHLIGHTS*

Turned Pro: 1987
PGA Wins: 2 (1 major)
First PGA Win: 2004
Best Season-end Placing: 11th (2004)
Ryder Cup: 0
Presidents Cup: 0

reason, 2004 turned out to be his special year. He finally got his card in December 2003 at Q-school after a great season in which he won four more events in Japan, and in 2004 he devoted himself to the PGA.

Prior to 2004, Hamilton had played just 12 PGA Tour events, but in his sixth start that year, he won for the first time in the U.S., taking the Honda Classic with a clutch performance down the stretch. He started the final day with a four-shot lead, only to see Davis Love III close the gap. However, Hamilton birdied the 17th and 18th holes to win by a stroke.

Soon after, he traveled to Royal Troon in Scotland to play in just his fourth appearance in the British Open. He had missed the cut in 1992, finished 44th in 1996 and missed the cut again in 2003. But in 2004, Hamilton found himself leading the tournament after 54 holes with a threesome of superstars chasing him. Ernie Els was a single shot off, and Retief Goosen and Phil Mickelson were just two back. Hamilton was in control all of the last day until the final hole. He bogeyed the 18th to fall into a tie with Els who finished birdie-birdie to force a four-hole playoff. Hamilton made par at all four holes while Els bogeyed the third, giving Hamilton a major championship in his rookie season.

In all, Hamilton won more than $3 million in 2004, finished 11th on the money list and was named Rookie of the Year. Not bad for a 38-year-old with 14 worldwide wins under his belt. Yet, just as quickly as he rose to the top, Hamilton fell to the bottom. He made only 17 of 31 cuts in 2005 and

fell to 134th on the money list, and, the year after, he made just 8 of 27 tournament cuts. In 2006, he even played a number of events on the European Tour, with just as little success. Things got worse in 2007. He missed the cut in 15 of 18 tournaments he entered to start the year, and finished no higher than 66th (at the Memorial in June).

The psychological makeup of a player is so intrinsic to his ability to win that the slightest increase or decrease in confidence can make a huge difference in a player's swing and temperament. For Hamilton, whatever he did right in 2004 has all but left him, and only he knows whether he has the ability to reclaim the lost magic of his golden season. ∎

CHARLES *HOWELL III*

Born: Augusta, Georgia, June 20, 1979

There's something wrong with anyone who grows up in the shadow of one of the world's pre-eminent tournaments and isn't interested in golf — and there's nothing wrong with Charles Howell III. Raised a stone's throw from Augusta National, home of the green-jacket Masters, he was shooting par by the time he was 10 years old. His career has gone up and up since then and has only sunshine and rainbows in its future.

Howell turned pro in the summer of 2000 after a spectacular college career at Oklahoma State University. He was buoyed by a second-place finish at the Greensboro Open (a Nationwide Tour event) while still an amateur, and after receiving special temporary member status on the PGA Tour, he continued to climb quickly. In 13 events before the end of the year, he made the cut in seven and earned more than $260,000. The next season he was named Rookie of the Year and earned his Tour card full-time.

That 2001 season saw him make 20 of 24 cuts. He lost to Shigeki Maruyama in a playoff at the Greater Milwaukee Open, but he did so after carding a birdie at six of the last seven holes to tie for the lead. In all, he earned more than $1.5 million. The next year, Howell continued to improve. He won his first tournament, the Michelob Championship, and had seven top-10 finishes to end the year ninth on the money list.

But a strange thing happened on the way to the top. Howell played some magnificent golf regularly but, all too regularly, there was one other player who played just a hair better. The result was a string of runner-up finishes and an almost five-year gap between victories.

In 2003, he lost the Nissan Open in a playoff to Mike Weir after blowing a three-shot lead and

CAREER *HIGHLIGHTS*

Turned Pro: 2000

PGA Wins: 2

First PGA Win: 2002

Best Season-end Placing: 9th (2002)

Ryder Cup: 0

Presidents Cup: 2

then was again bridesmaid, this time to Vijay Singh at the Tour Championship. In 2004, he shot an opening-round 61 to take the early lead at the Booz Allen Classic, but again finished second. In all, he finished second nine times between the Michelob victory and his next win, at the Nissan Open, in February 2007.

That win was a passionate one for young Howell. He defeated Phil Mickelson in a playoff just a week after finishing runner-up again. In defeating Mickelson, he also beat a top player who had won his last start, that at Pebble Beach. Howell's win was earned, to be sure, but it had a fair bit of luck to go with it. He was four shots off the lead with just eight holes to go, and although he shot a superb 65, he was aided by some bad misses from Mickelson who could have sealed the victory with any of a series of short putts. To wit, Mickelson missed a two-foot par putt on the

13th and a four-foot putt at the 16th. In the end, they went to a playoff, and on the fifth extra hole, Mickelson missed his par putt and Howell made his. A certain victory for Mickelson turned into defeat, and Howell was right there to claim first place with some excellent clutch putting.

Despite his geographic proximity to Augusta National as a kid, Howell has never played particularly well at the Masters. His best finish was a tie for 13th in 2004, and he hasn't fared much better at the other majors. He made the 2003 Presidents Cup team based on his standing on tour, winning three and losing two matches. But Howell remains one of the PGA's bright lights. He is still well shy of his 30th birthday and has already won more than $15 million. He is often in the thick of things on Sunday, but he has to find that last gear, the one that puts him ahead of his adversaries instead of one place behind. ■

Although injuries have become an ever-present part of David Howell's career, he remains one of the more successful international golfers in the world, maintaining an impressive record both on the PGA and European Tours simultaneously. And, indeed, his injuries might well have helped catapult him to the elite of the golf world.

Howell turned pro in 1995 before his 20th birthday, but for three years accumulated very little in tangible evidence to suggest he was a top golfer. His breakthrough came when he clobbered the field to win the 1998 Australian PGA Championship by a whopping seven shots. A year later, he won the Dubai Desert Classic and was on his way to worldwide fame.

Although it would be another six years before he won again, Howell made strides nonetheless. He continued to climb in the world rankings and in the European Tour's Order of Merit (money list), but injuries slowed him down. In 2002, he broke his arm while, of all things, jogging. In 2004, he moved into 10th spot on the European Tour, winning more than $3 million and finishing in the top-25 a staggering 17 times.

His tremendous play earned him a spot playing for the Europeans at the Ryder Cup, and he didn't disappoint. In the Saturday morning fourball matches, he teamed with Paul Casey to rally for a critical victory. The pair was 1-down with two holes to play, but won the 17th and 18th holes to steal a critical point from the American team of Jim Furyk and Chad Campbell. Although Howell lost his Sunday singles match to Furyk, 6-and-4, the Europeans easily won the trophy.

The 2005 season produced further success. Howell won the BMW International Open, beating John Daly and Brett Rumford, but he also missed two months with an abdominal injury. Howell began to take even greater effort to look after his body. He focused on fitness training, hired a physiotherapist and personal trainer, and worked toward making his body as healthy as possible to maintain a high level of play on the course.

As a result, Howell accomplished the rare double of finishing in the top 125 on the PGA Tour (to earn his full-time card for the next year) and also finished seventh overall in Europe. His 2005 season flowed seamlessly into 2006 with a confidence-building win in November at the Champions tournament in Shanghai, an event that counted toward the 2006 season. In that event, he was paired with Tiger Woods as the final group on the final day and bettered Woods by three strokes. The win catapulted him to another tremendous, dual season. Howell also won the BMW Championship by five strokes over Simon Khan, and he made 13 of 14 cuts on the PGA Tour. He also went undefeated (2–0–1) at the 2006 Ryder Cup and finished a career-high third on the European Tour Order of Merit.

Players must participate in 15 PGA Tour events in order to maintain their card from one year to the next, so Howell played in the Frys.com Open in Las Vegas toward the end of the season as his 15th appearance. He had to withdraw because of a shoulder injury, and in 2007 he missed two more months with a back injury. As a result, his 2007 season was a bit of a dog's breakfast, but when healthy he has proved to be among the best golfers in the world. Oddly, his greatest weakness is the four major championships, most notably his country's own British Open. In eight tournaments, he has missed the cut six times and finished woefully out of contention the other two times. In the U.S., his best result by a long shot was his 11th place showing at the 2005 Masters. ▪

CAREER *HIGHLIGHTS*

Turned Pro: 1995
PGA Wins: 0
First PGA Win: 0
Best Season-end Placing: 96th (2006)
Ryder Cup: 2
Presidents Cup: 0

ZACH *JOHNSON*

Born: Iowa City, Iowa, February 24, 1976

"I'm Zach Johnson, and I'm from Cedar Rapids, Iowa. That's about it. I'm a normal guy." Context is all, and Johnson uttered those simple but immortal lines under the most extraordinary circumstances of all, wearing a green jacket after having defeated Tiger Woods and the rest of the field to win the 2007 Masters. It was a shocking result, both for Johnson and Woods.

Johnson was a most unexpected champion, even in his own eyes. In a field studded with the greatest stars of the game, though, he produced a superb round in tough weather conditions on Sunday to win his first major championship. When Johnson woke up Sunday morning, Stuart Appleby was the leader by one stroke over Woods and 2-up on Johnson. Although Woods was the most dominant golfer in the game, he has had one black mark on his incomparable résumé — he had never won a major when trailing after 54 holes. But surely one shot was nothing major to overcome?

Indeed, Tiger took the lead early on when Appleby faltered badly, but Johnson hung in there and made some birdies when it mattered. Incredibly, Woods faltered, and Johnson made three birdies in four holes on the final nine to finish with a 69, beating Woods, Retief Goosen and Rory Sabbatini by two strokes. His +1 total tied the Masters record for highest winning score set in 1956. No matter. As victory seemed within reach, "the guy from Iowa" had gone about his business with a calm that belied his circumstance. During the championship ceremony, the 2006 winner, Phil Mickelson, put the green jacket on Johnson, and a new chapter in golf history was written.

Johnson's rise on tour has been steady and fairly rapid. After turning pro in 1998, he played two years on the little-known Prairie Golf Tour. He graduated to the Nationwide Tour and also played on the Hooters Tour, producing a record year on the Nationwide in 2003. That season,

CAREER *HIGHLIGHTS*

Turned Pro: 1998

PGA Wins: 3 (1 major)

First PGA Win: 2004

Best Season-end Placing: 7th (2007)

Ryder Cup: 1

Presidents Cup: 1

Johnson led the Tour in winnings with a record of nearly half a million dollars. He won twice and had 11 top-10 finishes and earned his PGA Tour card for 2004.

As a rookie in 2004, Johnson won his first tournament, the BellSouth Classic, coming up with a nervous win on Sunday which saw him card five birdies and four bogeys to win by a stroke. He won nearly $2.5 million that year and jumped from 207 to 41 in the world rankings. Although 2005 wasn't an improvement, he played steadily enough to know in his own heart that he was a bona fide Tour player.

Johnson had two runner-up appearances in 2006 and played consistently at a high level. Although he didn't win a tournament, he did qualify for the Ryder Cup where he posted a decent 1–2–1 record on a U.S. team that was slaughtered by the Europeans. But it was 2007 that brought him to the fore. In addition to his Masters win, Johnson also won the AT&T Classic with a clutch putt in a playoff. He and Ryuji Imada both finished at –15 for 72 holes, but on the first playoff hole, a par 5, Imada hit his second shot into the water while Johnson missed his eagle putt by inches. He tapped in for birdie to win. All three of his Tour victories have so far come in the State of Georgia.

Johnson isn't flashy or spectacular in any way. He dresses simply, plays with no flair, and isn't chunky, strong, tall, or short. He simply executes with the best of them and keeps his cool under pressure. Truly, he really is just a guy from Iowa — but he's one amazing golfer as well. ∎

SHAUN *MICHEEL*

Born: Orlando, Florida, January 5, 1969

Perseverance, thy name is Shaun Micheel. Micheel is virtually a self-taught golfer who came out of nowhere to win the 2003 PGA Championship, who faltered badly soon after, and then recovered to become a player to reckon with once again.

Although he turned pro in 1992, it was a decision he made fully a year after graduating from Indiana University, not the traditional method by any stretch. Even odder was the fact that he didn't get a proper foot in the PGA Tour door until 2000, by which time he had seen everything from the Asian to the Nationwide Tour to a series of mini-tours and a year in South Africa. Along the way, he also earned an award for bravery.

While driving to a tournament near New Bern, North Carolina, another stop on the mini-tour, he saw a car skid off the road and into a river. Micheel calmly pulled over, undressed to his knickers, and swam out to pull the couple to safety. Ironically, because of Micheel's inability to avoid water hazards during his final round, he ended up losing the very tournament he was driving to when rescuing the couple from their water hazard.

Micheel spent most of 1994–99 bouncing

CAREER *HIGHLIGHTS*

Turned Pro: 1992

PGA Wins: 1 (1 major)

First PGA Win: 2003

Best Season-end Placing: 32nd (2003)

Ryder Cup: 0

Presidents Cup: 0

between the Nationwide Tour and the PGA Tour, with occasional forays to the Far East for good measure. But he never felt comfortable in the limelight, never was at ease with crowds and traveling and playing the pressure game. He earned his PGA Tour card for the first time for 1994, but then made only four of 19 cuts and was right back on the Nationwide Tour. This pattern repeated itself frequently until 1999, when he had a great year on the Nationwide Tour and used this as a springboard to the PGA Tour once and for all. He won his first tournament that year, the Greensboro Open, and there were many encouraging signs from his first full year on the PGA Tour in 2000.

Micheel had three top-10 placings and made nearly half a million dollars, but a poor 2001 season (largely because of kidney-stone troubles) forced him back to Q-school. Undaunted, he qualified right away and was back on the PGA Tour in 2002 where he finished in the money in 21 of 30 events. Micheel stunned the golf world in 2003 when he won the PGA Championship in only his third appearance in a major. (Previously, he had missed the cut at the U.S. Open in 1999, and in 2001 he tied for 40th at the same event.)

He led the field after 36 holes of the 2003 PGA, and was tied with Chad Campbell after 54 holes, setting up a pressure-filled Sunday to which he responded with sublime calm. The two played in the final pairing and were close the entire day, leading up to the 18th hole. Micheel, with a one-shot lead in the fairway, sent his 175-yard approach shot to within inches of the cup, tapped in for birdie, and won the tournament by two strokes.

In all, Micheel had four top-10 finishes in 2003 before falling into a state of inconsistency. In 2004, for instance, he made the cut in all four majors, but then missed the cut in his next six majors over the following year and a half. The rest of the time was equally troubling. In 2005, he ended up a lowly 146th on the money list and used his exemptions from the PGA win to play many of his tournaments in 2006. At that year's PGA, he finished in second place, five shots behind Tiger Woods, giving himself a great payday and a much-needed shot of confidence. In 2007, he showed signs of coming to life, but sometimes missed the cut playing uninspired golf.

Micheel takes after his father and enjoys piloting planes in his free time, hoping one day to make his way around the Tour in his own plane to save the various hassles associated with 21st-century travel. It would be an appropriate metaphor for a player who has flown sky high after having scraped his nose along the ground in the early years of his career. ∎

JOHN ROLLINS

Born: Richmond, Virginia, June 25, 1975

John Rollins is one of those anonymous, ever-present names that shows up on the leaderboard every week, a name identified with always putting up a good fight and challenging the leaders but often falling just short.

A skilled and consistent golfer, Rollins has gone through the stages to play on the PGA Tour with seeming ease, and for his efforts he has made more than $8 million since turning pro in 1997. After graduating from Virginia Commonwealth University, Rollins played on the Nationwide Tour before placing high enough at Q-school to go to the PGA Tour for 2000. A dismal season, which saw him make only 8 of 27 cuts, landed him back in the Nationwide Tour, but he qualified again in 2001 and has been on top ever since.

Rollins came out to play in 2002, and unlike most PGA golfers, he played often. In all, he signed up for 34 tournaments and came away with his first win, the Canadian Open, in dramatic style. He shot a 65 on the last day and made it into a three-way playoff, thanks to a bit of luck. Neal Lancaster stood on the 72nd tee with a two-shot

CAREER HIGHLIGHTS

Turned Pro: 1997

PGA Wins: 2

First PGA Win: 2002

Best Season-end Placing: 25th (2002)

Ryder Cup: 0

Presidents Cup: 0

lead, but the pressure got to him and he double-bogeyed to allow Rollins and Justin Leonard into a playoff. On the first extra hole, Rollins scored the only birdie and in the process won one of the most prestigious events on the Tour.

In all, Rollins had six top-10 finishes that year and ended up 25th on the money list. His 2003 season was almost as good. He had a couple of leads late in tournaments but failed to win, yet held steady his position on the Tour. He dipped noticeably over the next two seasons, though, playing that anonymous-style golf only too well.

The 2006 and 2007 seasons saw Rollins rebound with a vengeance. In 2006, he won the B.C. Open by one stroke — producing great shots under pressure. His final-round 64 was capped by a birdie on the final hole to defeat Bob May by the slimmest of margins. In 2007, Rollins had a career year in many respects. In his third event of the season, he lost in a playoff at the Bob Hope Classic and two weeks later he again finished second, this time at the FBR Classic.

In the Bob Hope Classic, he birdied the final hole to get into a playoff with Charlie Hoffman, but on the first extra hole he hit an errant tee shot and had to scramble for par while Hoffman made birdie. In the case of the FBR, only bad luck prevented him from getting into another playoff. Standing in the 18th fairway on Sunday and trailing Aaron Baddeley by one shot, Rollins hit a sensational approach which hit the pin. Unluckily, instead of bouncing in or landing close, the ball skipped off the green and Rollins had to settle for par and second place, one shot behind Baddeley.

Despite his skill and modest success, Rollins has yet to qualify for a Ryder Cup or Presidents Cup team, and his play in the majors has been weak. His tie for 20th at the 2007 Masters has been by far his best result, missing six cuts in 13 majors appearances.

Rollins is not a spectacular golfer in any way. He is simply a solid Tour pro, making him one of the best in the world. Reliable, with a calm personality and steady swing, Rollins will likely never be a top-10 golfer, but he will also likely never be a

golfer who struggles for his Tour card every year, either. He is simply there, on tour, on the course, every day, making life potentially miserable for his opponents if they don't play their best. ■

JUSTIN ROSE

Born: Johannesburg, South Africa, July 30, 1980

The debate between long-term planning and short-term gain provides some unique answers through the career of Justin Rose, who turned professional at the tender age of 17 and has yet to win on the PGA Tour.

His last day as an amateur was surely one of the most memorable in modern golf. Playing in the 1998 British Open at Royal Birkdale, Rose holed his pitch shot on the tricky 18th and final hole of the championship to earn a tie for fourth, a remarkable score for a teenager. He earned the Silver Medal as top amateur in the field, and the next day he turned pro despite officially having a handicap of three.

Early success was nothing new to him. He scored a hole-in-one at age 10 and was a scratch golfer by his mid-teens. But he could never anticipate the hardships that awaited him as a moneymaker. For the next several years, Rose did very little to suggest his ambitions were merely the breezy dreams of idle youth. He had to qualify for his European Tour card, and once on course with the big boys he was no match.

It wasn't until 2002 that Rose started to realize his potential. He won the Dunhill Championship near the beginning of the season and followed with wins at the Masters Championship in South Africa, the Crowns Tournament in Japan, and the British Masters. The young star finally seemed to have established a reputation which, until then, had been founded entirely on one chip shot as a 17-year-old.

In 2003, Rose played 11 events on the PGA Tour and made nine cuts. Included in these were his first two major appearances in the U.S. He was a distant 39th at the Masters, but his tie for fifth at the U.S. Open was an impressive performance, to be sure.

Since then, he has continued to improve and victory on the PGA Tour seems imminent. Rose has made the PGA his full-time career since 2004 and his world rank has risen steadily in the process. He was the leader after the first and second rounds of the Masters in 2004, but an 81 on Saturday

CAREER HIGHLIGHTS

Turned Pro: 1998

PGA Wins: 0

First PGA Win: 0

Best Season-end Placing: 16th (2007)

Ryder Cup: 0

Presidents Cup: n/a

scrapped his chances that year. He finished fourth at the Canadian Open, and in 2005 he had two third-place finishes.

Rose started the 2006 PGA year by winning the Australian Masters, and he continued to improve on the PGA as well, coming home with five top-10 finishes. In 2007, he started the year by making all nine cuts and producing some impressive stats, notably a third-place finish at the Bob Hope Classic, a fifth at the Masters, and a 10th-place finish at the U.S. Open. What seems clear is that Rose is capable of playing with the best for two or three rounds but has yet to put four rounds together in one tournament. He has allowed early leads to slip away and doesn't yet have that killer instinct or the skill to get better on Sunday when the tournament is on the line.

Still, Rose seems to have defied the odds. So often a player who turns pro early crashes and burns and disappears. Rose seems to have come through the proverbial slaughter and shows signs of becoming one of the best young golfers around, even though at 27 he has 10 years of pro golf under his belt already. ■

ADAM SCOTT

Born: Adelaide, Australia, July 16, 1980

The praise is both flattering and intimidating, the compliments sincere yet full of expectation. Along with colleague and foe Sergio Garcia, Adam Scott is called either the best player in the world under 30 years of age or the best player in the world who has yet to win a major. In any case, he is among the best of the best, a player who has the game to win every time he plays. Yet, so far, none of his dozen victories worldwide have earned him a place in history the way a win at, say, Augusta or Carnoustie would.

Scott turned pro in 2000 and earned his European Tour card for the following season in near-record time, simply by finishing high in the select tournaments he entered. In that first full season, he had a plan — to cut his teeth in Europe and around the world, and to prepare himself for the PGA Tour. In 2001, he finished 13th on the Order of Merit list in Europe and also won his first event as a pro, the PGA Championship of South Africa. He also ended the season among the top 50 golfers in the world, a distinction which earned him an invitation to play in the Masters the following year.

By 2003, Scott was ready to join the PGA Tour, not full-time, but with an increased schedule by way of taking that next step. He won for the first time in the U.S. in his 34th career start, taking the Deutsche Bank Championship by four shots over Rocco Mediate. It was an impressive win, fuelled by a round of 62 on Friday to give him a one-shot lead over Vijay Singh. Scott didn't rest on that score, though. He led by two after 54 holes and closed out with a 66 to fend off Mediate. His fine 2003 season also included a third-place finish in the Match Play Championship and a berth for the Internationals on the Presidents Cup team, the youngest player on either side.

The next year, in 2004, Scott won twice on the PGA Tour, establishing himself as a bona fide star capable of driving the ball a long way and making clutch putts under pressure. The first of those wins came at the Players Championship, where he took

CAREER HIGHLIGHTS

Turned Pro: 2000

PGA Wins: 5

First PGA Win: 2003

Best Season-end Placing: 3rd (2006)

Ryder Cup: 0

Presidents Cup: 3

a comfortable lead and turned it into a nerve-racking finish. Scott stood at the 72nd tee with a two-stroke lead over Padraig Harrington, but he hooked his long approach shot into the water. That left him with 39 yards left to the pin, but he made a good chip and a determined putt from 10 feet to save a bogey and win by a single stroke. It wasn't pretty, as they say, but Scott showed good concentration and powers of recovery when he needed them the most.

His other win in '04 came at the Booz Allen Classic, but then he went another year without victory. In 2005 he earned $864,000 for one hole's worth of play at the Nissan Open. Tied with Chad Campbell after 36 holes, the weekend was rained out entirely. Tournament officials held a playoff on Monday between the two, and Scott won on the first extra hole to take home the first prize.

The 2006 season ended with Scott winning the Tour Championship, a prestigious and lucrative event that launched him to number four in the world rankings. Since then, he has maintained status in the top 10, most recently with a win at the 2007 Houston Open. Oddly, he won in similar fashion to his win at the Players Championship, putting a ball in the water on the final hole and scrambling for victory, this time thanks to a phenomenal 40-foot putt that turned and twisted its path into the cup.

Scott's game is as good as it gets. His swing is technically sound; he is strong, with a great sense of touch around the greens; and he has the nerves and ambition to want to win. He may be the "best golfer without a major," but that is a title he is not likely to have for very long. He will win, and he will win big. Of that there is no doubt. ■

CAMILO *VILLEGAS*

Born: Medellin, Colombia, January 7, 1982

He has yet to flick a steel-strong spiderweb from his wrists or fling himself from one tall Manhattan skyscraper to another, but Camilo Villegas nonetheless has rightfully earned the nickname Spider-Man. In his case, the designation is appropriate only because of what he does on the green.

Most players line up a putt in a similar manner. They crouch down, walk a circumference around their ball and the hole, perhaps use the putter to eye the line of the putt. Not Villegas. He adopts a pseudo-spider, pseudo-curler position by stooping down on one foot, extending the other leg fully out behind him, holding the putter in one hand and placing only the fingertips of his other hand on the green for balance, and getting a worm's-eye view of the path his ball will take. The contortion leaves most of his body parallel to the ground just a few inches above the grass, but it hasn't seemed to give him any advantage as he has yet to win on the PGA Tour.

Beyond his unique putting preparations, Villegas is young, good-looking and everything the PGA is looking for in a pinup player. He has bulging muscles and wears shirts to show the ripples; he drives the ball a mile, as they say, and the galleries love him. But so far, his career has been more Anna Kournikova than Maria Sharapova. That is, lots of fluff and photos, but no wins. That's not true entirely. As an amateur, Villegas had an outstanding career at the University of Florida. He was an All-American each of his four years, Player of the Year twice, and an eight-time winner. In 2001, while still a teen, he also won the Colombian Open.

Since turning pro in 2004, Villegas has moved up the ladder successfully and is now a full-time member of the PGA Tour. He played several events

that year on the PGA through sponsors' exemptions, but despite making 5 of 10 cuts, he had to go to the Nationwide Tour for 2005. By finishing 13th on that tour's money list, he qualified to join the PGA in 2006, and it was there the rookie introduced his style to the top level of the golf world.

His rookie season was impressive even without a win. Villegas finished second at both the FBR Open and the Ford Championship, and he had moments of success which he was unable to finish. He shared the second-round leadership at the Canadian Open, for instance, and finished in a tie for fifth after weekend rounds of 68 and 69. He shared the lead at the Ford Championship before succumbing to Tiger Woods on Sunday.

In 2007, he came even closer to winning. At the 2007 Honda Classic, he and three others — Mark Wilson, Jose Coceres and Boo Weekley—were tied after 72 holes. Villegas got there by making birdies at the 16th and 17th holes, responding well to the pressure of the day's events. At the second extra hole, though, Villegas and Weekley bogeyed and were eliminated, and two holes later Wilson defeated Coceres. Still, this was the closest Villegas got to winning. Later in the year he tied for third place at the AT&T Classic, another close-but-no-cigar result.

Villegas is still young by golf standards, and his skill is such that victory seems only a matter of time. For now, he plays every week to throngs of crowds with a large female component who cheer his big drives and hoot as he crouches down to line up a putt. Spider-Man on the green. ∎

CAREER *HIGHLIGHTS*

Turned Pro: 2004

PGA Wins: 0

First PGA Win: 0

Best Season-end Placing: 24th (2007)

Ryder Cup: n/a

Presidents Cup: 0

INTERNATIONAL
STARS

5

Although the PGA Tour in the U.S. is the top tour in the world, the numerous national tours overseas are loaded with great talent. Many players from those tours come to the U.S. to test themselves against the best, sometimes only a couple of times a year, sometimes more frequently. Regardless, their game measures up perfectly well against the average PGA Tour player and, as often as not, an international star plays four solid rounds and defeats the best the U.S. tour can offer. The international flavour is an important ingredient in golf — part wild card, part entertaining. To be sure, the players are as skilled as those on the PGA Tour — only less heralded.

Top (L-R): Colin Montgomerie, Henrik Stenson, Darren Clarke, Geoff Ogilvy
Bottom: Padraig Harrington

It took Angel Cabrera nearly two decades of professional golf to win a big tournament, but when he did, it was a doozy. Cabrera fought off Tiger Woods and Jim Furyk to win the 2007 U.S. Open at Oakmont Golf Club in Pennsylvania, becoming the first Argentine in 40 years to win the toughest test of golf. Appropriately, he won with nerves not of steel but of putty. He smoked cigarettes between shots, chatted amiably with his caddy, and stood over the ball for mere seconds before making one clutch shot after another. It was an impressive performance, indeed.

Oakmont played so tough all week that only eight times did players break par over the four days. Cabrera was responsible for two of those rounds, but early on he was more famous for knocking Phil Mickelson out of the tournament. Cabrera was the leader after 35 holes, and his approach shot to the final hole of day two landed inches from the cup. He tapped in for birdie, setting the cut line at +10 instead of +11 (Mickelson's score), forcing Mickelson to miss the cut.

Cabrera dropped back after a 76 on Saturday, but he was the last man standing on a crazy Sunday. On a day with treacherous pin placements and greens so fast it was like "putting on a balloon," in the words of pro-turned-analyst Roger Maltbie, six men had the lead at various points of the afternoon. Aaron Baddeley, playing in the final group, blew up right away to lose the lead. Stephen Ames made a couple of birdies to take the lead quickly before relinquishing it after a triple bogey and double bogey on consecutive holes. Steve Stricker, in the year of his renaissance, putted his way to the top before falling hard.

Cabrera, known as El Pato (the Duck) to his colleagues because of his stature and waddle of a walk, hit the ball long and straight throughout the tournament. He seemed pressure-proof all of Sunday, until bogeys at the 16th and 17th holes

put him into a tie with Furyk and only one ahead of Woods. But, so often at the U.S. Open, par is like birdie, and after making a four on the 18th hole, Cabrera went to the scorer's tent and watched the field come home. Furyk promptly bogeyed the 17th, and Woods stood at the 18th tee needing a birdie to tie Cabrera. A perfect drive and approach left him with a tricky 30-foot putt for birdie and a playoff, but he missed, and Caddie Eddie Gardino leaped into Cabrera's arms in celebration. Cabrera had his name on the championship trophy.

Previously, Cabrera had never challenged for a major; in 29 appearances, he missed the cut nine times and had just four top-10 finishes. He had

won several tournaments around the globe, but the U.S. Open win was his first on the PGA Tour.

His is a remarkable story. As a kid, he quit school to find a job and support his family, but his natural talent in golf was too difficult to ignore. Golfer Eduardo Romero, a neighbor in Cordoba, provided financial assistance to allow Cabrera to work on his game, and before his 20th birthday he had turned pro and was traveling the world playing golf. Cabrera missed gaining his European Tour card three times, and his first victory didn't come until 1995, when he won the Paraguay Open. Since then, he has won some 15 times around the world, in South America, Europe, and now the U.S.

His dedication to the game is rooted in his international status. To this day, Cabrera never plays more than a dozen or so events on the PGA Tour, content with earning special exempt status for part of the year while he plays in his native Argentina, as well as on the European Tour. In 1999, he tied for fourth at the British Open, and he has had three top-10 finishes at the Masters.

He made his first Presidents Cup team in 2005 where he had a record of 1-1-3. He coupled with fellow U.S. Open champ, New Zealand's Michael Campbell, during the foursomes and fourball

events, and Cabrera notably halved with Phil Mickelson on the final day in singles after the tournament had been decided. Cabrera made the Presidents Cup team again in 2007, finishing with a 2-2-1 record.

Like John Daly, Jason Gore and Bubba Watson, Cabrera doesn't spend much time in the gym or on the practice range. Instead he hits the long ball and trolls the fairways lighting one cigarette after another. He champions a casual approach to the game, which has, for him, sometimes ended in heartbreak. Known for squandering leads under pressure, Cabrera helped shed that stigma with Oakmont 2007, the most important lead he's retained of his entire career. ■

CAREER *HIGHLIGHTS*

Turned Pro: 1989

PGA Wins: 1 (1 major)

First PGA Win: 2007

Best Season-end Placing: 47th (2007)

Ryder Cup: n/a

Presidents Cup: 2

DARREN *CLARKE*

Born: Dungannon, Northern Ireland, August 14, 1968

More than any other athletes, golfers have always maintained a strict separation between their public life and their private life. It is only rarely that fans get a glimpse behind the clubs, so to speak, and one of those glimpses was the sad tale of Darren Clarke and his wife Heather, who died of cancer in the summer of 2006 at just 39 years of age.

A colorful and well-liked member of the golfing fraternity, Clarke missed much of 2005 and 2006, attending to his ailing wife. It was a time of mourning for a player known for his broad smile, love of cigars and *joie de vivre*. Clarke left the Tour after missing the cut at the 2006 British Open in June and didn't return to the game until after his wife's death. His first tournament back was the Ryder Cup in late September. He was named to the team by captain Ian Woosnam and responded with an emotional performance, winning all three matches including his singles match, 3-and-2, over Zach Johnson.

Clarke was just 22 years old when he turned pro in 1990 after winning three prestigious international amateur titles that year. He played exclusively in Europe for the first four years of his career and eased into life on the PGA Tour in succeeding years. His first significant result came at the 1997 British Open where he finished in a tie for second place with Jesper Parnevik, three shots behind winner Justin Leonard. By this time, Clarke had won twice in Europe: at the 1993 Alfred Dunhill Open and the Linde German Masters in 1996.

The British Open has proved to be Clarke's favorite of the four majors, largely because it's played on a links course the likes of which he grew up on and learned the game on. In 2000, he tied for seventh, and the next year he finished tied for third, by far his best results. In all, Clarke

CAREER *HIGHLIGHTS*

Turned Pro: 1990

PGA Wins: 2

First PGA Win: 2000

Best Season-end Placing: 28th (2004)

Ryder Cup: 5

Presidents Cup: n/a

has only three other top-10 finishes at the majors, including a tie for eighth at the 1998 Masters, a tie for ninth at the PGA Championship in 2000 and a tie for tenth at the U.S. Open in 1999.

In Europe, Clarke has finished second on the Order of Merit (for earnings) four times. His first sensational year, though, was 2000 when he won the Match Play Championship, defeating David Duval in the semifinals and Tiger Woods in the finals. Later that year, he won the English Open.

Clarke's next big season came in 2003 when he won the World Golf Championship, his second PGA victory. This was a year he played a career-high 16 events in the U.S., and as a result, his play in Europe suffered and he won only once back home, at the Northern Ireland Masters. He made the cut in 15 of those 16 events and finished 85th on the money list, impressive indeed, given his status as a part-time player.

An important part of his résumé consists of his Ryder Cup participation. He has played in every Ryder Cup since 1997, being on the losing side only once (1999). In 2004, he had a not-so-memorable event, losing four matches before halving with Davis Love III in singles play on the final day. This was in stark contrast to 2002 when he earned 3½ points and went undefeated in five matches. In 1999, he won all three of his matches including a 4-and-2 win over Hal Sutton on the final day of singles when the U.S. mounted one of the greatest comebacks in golf history. In 1997, his first appearance in the Ryder Cup, he played only twice but won both matches, notably a 2-and-1 result over Phil Mickelson in singles play.

Since his return to golf after the passing of his wife, Clarke has had a difficult time. His focus has been more on raising his two young sons than traveling the world, and his play has suffered as a result, both in the U.S. and Europe. Time, no doubt, will heal the pain of loss, but until then, Clarke must take solace in his children and his abilities to play golf at a world-class level. ∎

PADRAIG *HARRINGTON*

Born: Dublin, Ireland, August 31, 1971

A golfer's career can very often be defined by specific shots played at specific times. He who plays well under pressure makes great shots; he who doesn't, doesn't. Padraig Harrington is now a part of golf's great history, thanks to his great play on the final day of the 2007 British Open, but his horrible gaffe late on that same day almost relegated him to the ash can of infamy and trivia instead. In the end, he came from six strokes back of leader Sergio Garcia on the final day to win his first major, but it wasn't as easy as it sounds.

While Garcia battled the gremlins in his head on that fateful day, Andres Romero was charging up the leaderboard with a succession of birdies, 10 in all on the Sunday. But both men faltered and Harrington, playing several groups ahead, made a steady climb with brilliant shotmaking. He stood on the 18th hole, the final hole, with a two-shot lead. The British Open was all but his. Then horror struck.

Harrington put his drive in the Barry Burn, a narrow, snaking water trench that wends its way through the final two holes. He took a drop and promptly put his third shot in another part of the Burn, further up hole. He wedged his fifth shot close and made his putt, but that left him one stroke behind Sergio Garcia, who stood at the 18th tee, needing only a par to win and sending Harrington to the Jean Van de Velde depths of despair (Van de Velde had a three-stroke lead in the 1999 British Open and lost it on the final hole).

Luckily for Harrington, Garcia bogeyed the final hole and the two went to a playoff, the best score over four holes being named winner. On the first extra hole, Harrington made a brilliant approach shot over hulking bunkers guarding the front of the green, and made his birdie putt. Garcia bogeyed, and after two par holes, they stood together at the 18th tee, Harrington with a two-stroke lead. This time, the leader took out an iron and played two cautious shots, put his third on the green and two-putted for a bogey to give him a one-stroke win and put himself in the history books.

Harrington and Garcia had met before in extra holes. They and Rory Sabbatini participated in a three-man playoff at the 2004 Buick Classic, won by Garcia, but in 2005, Harrington won the Honda Classic in a playoff with Vijay Singh. In

2006, Harrington did the unthinkable, winning the Order of Merit (money leader) in Europe while placing 68th on the PGA Tour where he had three top-10 finishes. He has also played in the last four Ryder Cup matches, with a winning record each year.

On a good day — and there have been many — Harrington can count himself among that quartet of golfers who are the very best in the world — Tiger Woods, Phil Mickelson and Ernie Els. His record on both the PGA and European Tours has been exemplary, but until 2007 it lacked the exclamation point that is a major tournament win.

After turning pro in 1995, Harrington played mostly in Europe for several years, though he steadily increased the PGA content of his schedule over that time until 2003, when things reversed — he became a full-time PGA player with part-time commitments to Europe.

It wasn't until 2005 that he won on the PGA Tour, but he proved himself to be an extraordinary big-time player. In the last ten years, he has had seven top-10 finishes in the four major tournaments, and he had back-to-back second-place finishes in the Players Championship in

2003 and 2004, the event most golfers consider the fifth major because of the strength of the field and the quality of the golf course (TPC Sawgrass). In 2002, Harrington was the only player to finish in the top 10 in three of the majors, and he finished 17th in the other (PGA). Yet, for all his great performances, it seemed there was always someone else who played just a little better.

The PGA Tour shot (on U.S. soil) for which he is most famous is certainly his final putt in the 2005 Barclays Classic. He and Jim Furyk stood at the 18th tee on Sunday tied, but Harrington sank a 66-foot eagle putt over a stretch of lawn that had as many twists and turns as the watery Barry Burn. It fell into the cup for the win. ∎

CAREER *HIGHLIGHTS*

Turned Pro: 1995

PGA Wins: 3 (1 major)

First PGA Win: 2005

Best Season-end Placing: 14th (2005)

Ryder Cup: 4

Presidents Cup: n/a

SHIGEKI *MARUYAMA*

Born: Chiba, Japan, September 12, 1969

Although his English still isn't very good, Shigeki Maruyama lets his golf swing do the talking most of the time. As a result, he is perfectly well understood wherever he plays.

Maruyama's career has two distinct phases to it. The first consists of the eight-year period, 1992–2000, when he developed his game in the comfort of his own home country, Japan. After graduating from Nihon University, he turned pro and spent those years on the Japan Golf Tour, quickly becoming one of the best golfers in a country and obsessed with the game. During these years, he made occasional forays to the PGA Tour, playing just often enough to get noticed.

Maruyama won nine tournaments during this stretch, but the highlight of his early years came in 1998 when he was named to the Presidents Cup team. Short, chunky and unassuming, with a broad smile and killer instinct, Maruyama led the International side to a dominating victory over the U.S. at the Royal Melbourne Golf Club in Australia.

Over the first two days of foursomes and fourball, he teamed with local favorite Craig Parry and countryman Joe Ozaki to win all four of his matches. On the final day of singles, he defeated John Huston 3-and-2 at a critical time, to win an astounding five points for his side. The next year, Maruyama earned his full-time playing card for

2000 after a series of high finishes at World Golf Championship events, and he made the most of his PGA Tour opportunity.

While most non-American golfers split their seasons between the PGA and home, Maruyama embraced the U.S. unconditionally, starting, metaphorically, with his trademark cowboy hat. He moved his family to Los Angeles and rarely played away from the PGA, and this dedication maximized his chance to succeed on the world's toughest tour.

In his rookie season, 2000, Maruyama had seven top-10 finishes and earned more than $1 million, notably a tie for second with Tiger Woods at the Buick Invitational. But the highlight of the year was a qualifying tournament for the U.S. Open at the unheralded Woodmont Country Club in Rockville, Maryland. Maruyama shot a 58, an unheard of score in golf. Ironically, after

CAREER *HIGHLIGHTS*

Turned Pro: 1992

PGA Wins: 3

First PGA Win: 2001

Best Season-end Placing: 16th (2002)

Ryder Cup: n/a

Presidents Cup: 2

this great effort, he went to the U.S. Open and missed the cut!

Maruyama recorded PGA Tour wins in three straight years from 2001 to 2003, starting with a playoff win over Charles Howell III at the Greater Milwaukee Open. With the win, he became the first Japanese player to win on the U.S. mainland. (Isao Aoki won in Hawaii in 1983.) Maruyama had the best year of his career in 2002. He won the Byron Nelson Classic, finished in a tie for fifth at the British Open, and teamed with Toshi Izawa to win the World Cup later in the year. In all, he finished 16th on the money list.

He completed his hat trick of wins at the Chrysler Classic in 2003. Although he hasn't won since, he continued to be consistently successful for the next several years. Maruyama had his worst year on the PGA in 2007. In his first 21

tournaments, he missed 10 cuts and withdrew from four other events for a variety of reasons, ranging from injury to poor play. He missed part of 2002 with a shoulder injury and was hampered by a neck injury early in 2003, but his slide in 2007 seemed to have been more than just physical. Nonetheless, he is too good a golfer to be down for too long.

Maruyama owns a course outside Tokyo which he runs in part to allow kids without financial means the opportunity to play. His father was a successful realtor, so as a boy Shigeki had no trouble playing when and where he wanted, but he knows not everyone with great golf skill is as fortunate. He also runs a junior golf foundation in Japan so, although he may have adopted the PGA as his home away from home, he has hardly forgotten who he is or where he comes from. ■

COLIN *MONTGOMERIE*

Born: Glasgow, Scotland, June 23, 1963

Colin Montgomerie's place in golf is complex and mysterious in many ways. He has been one of the premier golfers in the world for close to two decades and is arguably the greatest competitor in Ryder Cup history. On the other hand, he has never won a stroke tournament in the United States.

Montgomerie's total lack of success is odd, given that he was one of the first European players to pursue a career via a U.S. college, the traditional route for young Americans. He attended Houston

Baptist University but didn't enjoy it enough to stay for four years. He returned home, where he quickly became one of the dominant players on the European Tour.

He was named Rookie of the Year on the European Tour for 1988 and won his first tournament, the Portuguese Open, the next year. Between 1989 and 2007, he won at least one tournament almost every year. Montgomerie also led the European Tour in winnings for seven straight seasons, 1993–1999, the prize for which is known as the Order of Merit. He won for an eighth time in 2005.

Despite winning more than 30 tournaments in Europe, Montgomerie has never won on American soil. He is also considered to be the most accomplished active player who has never won a major championship either. Yet, he has been a runner-up five times, with some heartbreaking finishes. In 1994 at the U.S. Open, he was tied with Ernie Els and Loren Roberts after 72 holes, setting up a three-way, 18-hole playoff on the Monday. Montgomerie shot a 78 while his competitors shot 74, with Els eventually winning on the 20th hole. The next year, Montgomerie finished second at the PGA Championship, losing in another playoff, this time to Steve Elkington.

Another bitter defeat came at the 1997 U.S. Open. He was tied with Els on the 17th hole on Sunday but bogeyed the hole while Els parred the 18th to win. Perhaps most crushing was his loss at the 2006 U.S. Open. Standing at the 72nd hole with a one-stroke lead, he drove the ball perfectly down the middle of the fairway. His approach shot was short, however, his chip weak, and three putts later he walked off with a double bogey to finish a stroke behind winner Geoff Ogilvy.

Further complicating Montgomerie's poor play in the United States is his relationship with the galleries. He was loudly heckled by rude fans

at the 1997 U.S. Open and handled the situation badly, allowing the hecklers to affect his composure and play. He has been further jeered during Ryder Cup competition in the U.S., and it has only been very recently that he has been accorded the due respect given all other top golfers.

Paradoxically, Montgomerie's record in Ryder Cup play has virtually no equal. He has participated in eight competitions and posted a remarkable record of 20–9–7. More spectacularly, he is undefeated in singles play (6–0–2), arguably the toughest day of the Ryder Cup when the winner is decided and the pressure overwhelming. He has beaten the likes of Lee Janzen, Ben Crenshaw, Payne Stewart, Scott Hoch, and David Toms. In five of the eight Ryder Cups he has participated in, Europe has defeated the U.S.

Montgomerie's allegiance has always been first and foremost to the European Tour. He never stays in the U.S. for extended periods of time and never plays enough to be considered a full-time PGA Tour player. Yet he is one of the finest strikers of the ball in the world. What he seems to be lacking is the mettle to compete under intense pressure in PGA events, a pressure under which he thrives in match play competition. Truly, his is a complex and mysterious career. ∎

CAREER *HIGHLIGHTS*

Turned Pro: 1987

PGA Wins: 0

First PGA Win: 0

Best Season-end Placing: 37th (1997)

Ryder Cup: 8

Presidents Cup: n/a

GEOFF *OGILVY*

Born: Adelaide, Australia, June 11, 1977

On the cusp of joining that elite group that leads all golfers, Geoff Ogilvy is possessed of all aspects of the game to become the best of the best. His rise has been steady, consistent, and impressive, and the 2006 U.S. Open champion is due to see first place many more times before being put out to the Champions Tour pasture.

Ogilvy turned pro in 1998 and played in Australia and Europe for just three years before moving to the PGA Tour. He won his first title in the U.S. in 2005, winning the Chrysler Classic of Tuscon in a playoff. He got to extra holes with Mark Calcavecchia and Kevin Na. Calcavecchia went out in the first hole and Ogilvy birdied the second hole to better Na.

Ogilvy's win at Winged Foot Golf Course in 2006 will go down as one of the most remarkable finishes in U.S. Open history. To start the final round, he trailed Phil Mickelson and Kenneth Ferrie by one stroke. Ferrie fell off the pace during the day, but Mickelson and Ogilvy kept at it and were joined later in the day by Colin Montgomerie who was playing his best stroke-play golf of his career on American soil.

Ogilvy got to the clubhouse first with a score of +5 thanks to two brilliant shots on the 17th and 18th holes. In the case of the first, he chipped in for par, and in the second he made a great up-and-down for par. Behind him was Montgomerie, who stood at the 18th tee with a one-shot lead and a chance to win his first major. He made a

CAREER *HIGHLIGHTS*

Turned Pro: 1998
PGA Wins: 3 (1 major)
First PGA Win: 2005
Best Season-end Placing: 5th (2006)
Ryder Cup: n/a
Presidents Cup: 1

perfect drive, but his approach shot fell short of the green, and he fell apart, taking a double bogey to finish at +6.

Mickelson was the last golfer on the course, standing in the 18th tee box at +4 and a chance for a win. He sliced his drive badly and tried to reach the green with his second shot from a densely-treed area. The ball caromed off a tree and fell near where he was standing, and he gave the tournament away with a double bogey of his own on the last hole. Ogilvy, watching in the clubhouse, won the tournament that two men ahead of him should well have won.

Although he backed into the win, it was deserving and not surprising. Earlier in the year, Ogilvy won the Match Play Championship in extraordinary fashion. He was seeded 52nd in the 64-man field, but won five matches in a row to claim the win. Incredibly, his first four matches all went to extra holes, and time and again his opponents had chances to win but missed crucial putts. In the first round, Michael Campbell could have eliminated him but missed, and on the first extra hole Ogilvy chipped in for birdie and victory. In round two, Nick O'Hern missed a 4-foot putt that would have sent Ogilvy packing, but it was Ogilvy who got the last laugh on the third extra hole.

In the third round, he trailed Mike Weir by four holes after 14 and should have lost, but Weir had three opportunities to clinch the win and missed the deciding putt each time. Incredibly, Ogilvy managed to eagle the 21st hole to win.

In the 36-hole final, Ogilvy beat Davis Love III by 4-and-3. In all, he played 129 holes, a record for the tournament. In 2007, Ogilvy went the distance again, only to lose to Henrik Stenson in the finals by 2-and-1. It was the opposite of what had occurred in 2006, as Ogilvy missed several putts from close range at times when he could have drawn even. Stenson birdied the 35th and 36th holes to win.

Ogilvy has won three times in the last three years and is not done yet. He is young, talented, and a winner under pressure with an accurate drive, an essential part of setting up the rest of his game. His fairway play is exceptional, and his play around the greens is among the best in the world. The 2006 U.S. Open champion is sure to win another major during his career — the only question is when. ■

NICK O'HERN

Born: Perth, Australia, October 18, 1971

A world-class golfer, Nick O'Hern is most noticeable on the putting green. Here, the left-hander uses a belly putter, a unique combination in the world of golf. However, O'Hern is more famous for standing in the way of the world's number-one golfer than he is for any tournament victory. That is, O'Hern is the only man on the planet to have beaten Tiger Woods more than once in match play.

O'Hern grew up in Western Australia, where he was such a good baseball and tennis player in his youth that he wasn't sure which sport to focus on for a career. He eventually decided on golf. Turning pro in 1994 at age 22, he played for several years in Australia before trying the Nationwide Tour in the U.S. as a way to get to the PGA Tour. He had limited success and returned home. Back in Australia, O'Hern won once in each of three straight years (1997–99), and in 2001, he started to take his PGA aspirations more seriously. As a top-ranked world golfer, he was able to earn various exemptions in the U.S., and from there his strong finishes enabled him to compete more frequently.

The highlight of his 2001 season occurred during the World Match Play Championship which was being held in his native Australia. The then unheralded O'Hern pulled off three significant victories in that tournament, defeating the second seed in his group, Hal Sutton, in 21 holes, hammering Tim Herron 5-and-3, and finishing with an equally dominating win over Dudley Hart, 5-and-4. The magic run ended when Steve Stricker beat him in 20 holes (Stricker's only win in this format).

Over the next four years, O'Hern struggled to crack the PGA. He played some golf on the Nationwide Tour, but mostly played overseas. Starting in 2005, however, O'Hern was able to play close to full time on the PGA with special temporary member status because of his excellent play on the European Tour. That season marked the first time he played in all four majors. His best result was a tie for 15th at the British Open, and in 13 tournaments that year he made the cut 10 times. His finest moments of 2005, though, came in two match-play events.

In the first, O'Hern defeated Tiger Woods 3-and-1 in the second round of that year's Match Play Championship. He managed to get an early lead, winning the second and third holes, and despite the tenacity of Tiger, O'Hern held the number-one player at bay and clinched the match with a long birdie putt on the 17th hole.

O'Hern's other significant venture into match-play golf in 2005 was as a member of the International team in the Presidents Cup. He had the distinction of playing all five matches, winning twice and losing three times. On the first day, he and partner Tim Clark lost on the final hole to Phil Mickelson and Chris DiMarco in the foursomes. The next afternoon, in the fourball, he teamed with Peter Lonard to defeat Davis Love III and Kenny Perry, 3-and-2. Day three, a 36-hole marathon, saw O'Hern and Clark beat Fred Funk and David Toms 2-and-1 in foursomes in the morning, and in the afternoon he and Lonard were crushed by Mickelson and DiMarco, 6-and-5, in fourball. On the final day, in the singles matches, he lost to Love 4-and-3.

In 2006, O'Hern continued to improve. In just his second start at the U.S. Open, an event known for being the toughest tournament on the calendar, he finished in sixth place, and in December he earned his finest win up to that time, at the Australian Open. O'Hern showed tremendous mental fortitude in that event. He missed two routine putts late on Sunday which would have given him a victory — including one from inside three feet on the 72nd hole — but Peter Lonard played perfect golf that day and the pair had identical scores after 72 holes. On the

fourth hole of the playoff, O'Hern holed a shot from a greenside bunker to win.

O'Hern's second win over Tiger Woods came at the 2007 Match Play Championship at the La Costa Resort and Spa in Carlsbad, California, in February. O'Hern went 4-up after just seven holes on his way to what seemed like a crushing victory over the world's number-one player. But Woods made a tremendous charge to tie the match, setting the stage for a remarkable finish. O'Hern birdied the 17th hole to go 1-up, but Tiger responded in dramatic fashion, making birdie on the final hole while O'Hern three-putted to force extra holes. On the 20th hole, Woods missed his putt for par and O'Hern made his, sending Tiger packing. Officially, it ended Tiger's PGA Tour winning streak at seven, one of the longest streaks in Tour history. ■

CAREER *HIGHLIGHTS*

Turned Pro: 1994

PGA Wins: 0

First PGA Win: 0

Best Season-end Placing: 62nd (2007)

Ryder Cup: n/a

Presidents Cup: 2

Of course, any time a player wins one of golf's four majors, there is cause for joy, celebration and even a few tears. But for José Maria Olazabal, winning the 1999 Masters was not just special — it was a miracle. He had watched the 1998 Masters from his couch, unable to walk properly, fearing a life of decrepitude. Forget about golf. He thought a wheelchair was next.

The trouble started in 1995 when he withdrew from the Ryder Cup with problems in both feet. The diagnosis was rheumatoid polyarthritis. By the following year, the condition had not abated, so he visited German doctor Hans-Wilhelm Muller-Wohlfahrt, who traced the problem to a herniated disc in Olazabal's back that was affecting his feet. Olazabal started therapy, and after 18 months of nearly complete inactivity, he was soon up and walking, exercising and playing golf again. In late

1998, incredibly, he won the Dubai Open, his first win in four years.

In the 1999 Masters, the first major of his first full year back, Olazabal put together rounds of 70–66–73–71 to beat Davis Love III by two strokes, a win so improbable even Olazabal hadn't expected it. Not only did he bounce back from the injury, he improved his game in the years that followed. In 2002, he had arguably the best season of his career, winning twice and adding seven top-10 finishes to his list of accomplishments. In the U.S., he won the Buick Invitational, and overseas he won the Hong Kong Open.

The 1999 Masters win added to Olazabal's impressive status as one of the best Europeans in the tournament's history. He finished second in 1991, tied for seventh in 1993, finished fourth in 2002, and tied for third in 2006. Oh, yes, and he won in 1994, his first major victory. That year, he

CAREER *HIGHLIGHTS*

Turned Pro: 1985

PGA Wins: 6 (2 majors)

First PGA Win: 1990

Best Season-end Placing: 7th (1994)

Ryder Cup: 7

Presidents Cup: n/a

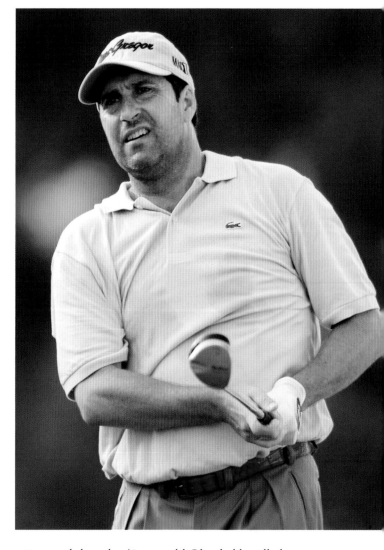

outduelled Tom Lehman who led Olazabal by one stroke heading into the final round. Lehman shot a 72 on Sunday while Olazabal responded with a 69. In all, Olazabal has finished in the top 10 some 13 times in major competition. Outside of the Masters, his best finishes came at the British Open (two third-place finishes, in 1992 and 2005) and the PGA Championship (tied for fourth in 2000). Despite three top-10 finishes at the U.S. Open, though, that tournament remains the one he has yet to contend in on the final day.

Olazabal's is a career that represents the best of the best. That is, his greatest moments, those that define his career and place him in the annals of the history of the sport, have come in the big tournaments — the majors and the Ryder Cup. No stage is too big or intimidating for him, no challenge too great.

After turning pro in 1985, Olazabal won in Europe for the first time a year later and in 1987, at age 21, he made his Ryder Cup debut. On Day One, European captain Tony Jacklin paired him with the great Seve Ballesteros and the two won both their first-day matches in foursomes and fourballs. They won another match the next day, starting, as Claude Rains said in *Casablanca,* "a beautiful friendship," that saw the pair compile a remarkable 11–2–2 record in pairs competition over the years.

History repeated itself in 2006 — just as he was the young gun in 1985 paired with the veteran Ballesteros, 2006 saw Olazabal play the veteran role with the youngster Sergio Garcia as his teammate. The pair won two matches in the early

going, and then the 40-year-old Olazabal handled world's number-two ranked Phil Mickelson 2-and-1 on the final day as part of the massive European victory over the U.S. It is the Ryder Cup where Olazabal has enjoyed continuous success. To date, he has an 18–8–5 record, including a perfect 3–0–0 record from the 2006 event.

Olazabal's best years might now be behind him, but his place in history is undeniable. From his early 1994 Masters win in his prime, to his remarkable comeback win in 1999 and his dominating performance in the Ryder Cup, his is a name to be talked about for generations to come as one of the best Spaniards ever to play the game and arguably one of the best golfers period, regardless of nationality. ▪

The burning question for Ian Poulter and his fans is whether they have already seen the best, or whether the frequent glimpses of greatness are signs of things to come. Indeed, it seems Poulter has more to give and more to accomplish than what he has done to date, but if that is the case, one wonders why he hasn't done more so far. He has the talent.

As a kid, Poulter was surrounded by golf. His father cut a 3-wood down to size for him, and his brother Danny also loved the game and became a fine player. They grew up not far from where Nick Faldo lived and were able to follow the great career of one of England's finest golfers of all time.

Poulter turned pro in 1995 at age 19 and joined the Challenge Tour, the lower circuit affiliated with the European Tour. He won his first tournament in 1999, the Cote d'Ivoire Open, but his season was cut short when he tripped over a golf bag and tore tendons in his ankle. The lengthy layoff affected his ranking, and he was forced back to Q-school.

In 2000, Poulter joined the European Tour and had an outstanding season. He was named Rookie of the Year and won the Italian Open, finishing 31st on the Order of Merit (European Tour money list). The next year he won again, this time at the Moroccan Open, and in 2002 he won the Italian Open for a second time.

It may not have been the turning point of his career, but 2003 saw Poulter win two events and start to take his career to a new level of success. He won the Wales Open and the Nordic Open, and finished fifth on the European money list. He also played four tournaments in the U.S. on the PGA Tour, making all four cuts, which gave him a taste of life on the PGA. The following year (2004), he played nine events after gaining temporary Tour member status in August.

Thus, 2004 was his breakout year. In addition to making a commitment to the PGA, he also was named to the Ryder Cup team, a team he had

CAREER HIGHLIGHTS

Turned Pro: 1995

PGA Wins: 0

First PGA Win: 0

Best Season-end Placing: 51st (2006)

Ryder Cup: 1

Presidents Cup: n/a

narrowly missed qualifying for in 2001. Poulter posted a 1–1 record for the victorious Europeans, and at the final European Tour event of the year he defeated Sergio Garcia in a playoff at the Volvo Masters. His first PGA event of the year was the Match Play Championship where he finished tied for fifth after losing 1-up to Stephen Leaney in the fourth round.

The next year, Poulter made it to the semifinals of the Match Play event and finished fourth. It was a season defined by his PGA life. For the first time in five years he failed to win in Europe, but in the U.S., he made nearly $1 million and finished 86th on the money list. He also played in all four majors for the first time, making the cut in all but the U.S. Open.

Poulter continued the difficult task of splitting his time between the U.S. and Europe in 2006, yet he finished ninth in Europe and 51st on the PGA money list, an impressive combination. His only win came in Spain at the Madrid Masters, and his next best finish was in London at the World Golf Championship, a PGA event.

Although he is not long off the tee, he is a reliable shot maker who has yet to show he can putt under great pressure — the sign of a great golfer. Poulter is known around the golfing world for his wacky and weird hairstyles and his even more eccentric wardrobe, wearing a variety of colorful, theme-based outfits which make him easily identifiable inside the ropes. Yet that flair for the sartorial has yet to be matched by a flair for dramatic shots and trophy holding that are the truer staples of a great golfer. ∎

HENRIK STENSON

Born: Gothenburg, Sweden, April 5, 1976

There seems to be unlimited potential for Henrik Stenson, a golfer who is getting better and better as he matures and learns the game with each succeeding season. He has paid the price along the way, though, and the man known as "Iceman" certainly has not always been nerveless and unflappable. No, he used to have plenty of nerves and flap, but through experience, frustration, and misery has learned to overcome obstacles.

Stenson was late to start at golf and didn't become a scratch player until he was 18. He didn't waste any time in improving, though. He went from the Swedish national junior team to senior team in one season (1994–1995) and ended his amateur career in 1998 playing for Sweden at the Eisenhower Trophy championship in Chile. The next year, he turned pro and started on the Challenge Tour, the European Tour's developmental level of play.

That first year as a pro (1999), Stenson played only seven times and had to return to the Challenge Tour for 2000. He became the dominant player, winning three times, finishing in the top 10 on five other occasions, and winning the money title. This earned him a promotion to the European Tour as a full-time member for 2001.

That year was the best and worst of times for Stenson. He won his first event, the Benson and Hedges International, but his game and mental makeup came apart at the K Club in Ireland during the European Open. After a disastrous nine holes, he walked to the clubhouse and withdrew from the tournament and took time to reassess his game. It was four years before he came back in any substantial way.

In the interim, he hired a coach, hit balls with his eyes closed, and relearned the game, as it

CAREER HIGHLIGHTS

Turned Pro: 1999

PGA Wins: 1

First PGA Win: 2007

Best Season-end Placing: 39th (2007)

Ryder Cup: 1

Presidents Cup: n/a

were. In 2005, Stenson had a significant impact on golf again. He had eight top-10 finishes on the European Tour and finished eighth on the Order of Merit. He also finished third at the World Golf Championship in San Francisco on the PGA Tour.

Stenson carried his fine play to another level in 2006, thanks in part to his recruitment of a new caddy. He hired Fanny Sunesson for his bag, the same Fanny who had caddied for Nick Faldo during several of Faldo's most successful years, and was a Swede who could understand Stenson's personality and speak to him in his native tongue. Stenson won twice on the European Tour, finished sixth on the Order of Merit and also finished in a tie for third at the Players Championship. And, he holed the putt that gave the Europeans victory in the Ryder Cup during his sound win over Vaughn Taylor by a 4-and-3 count.

The remarkable rise and turnaround was complete in 2007. Stenson started the year by winning two important tournaments. He won the Dubai Classic by one stroke over Ernie Els and two ahead of Tiger Woods, and then won the Match Play Championship. The Match Play event was played at the Gallery Golf Club in Tuscon, Arizona, and Stenson defeated Geoff Ogilvy 2-and-1 to win that 36-hole final. He had earlier defeated Zach Johnson, K.J. Choi, Aaron Baddeley, Nick O'Hern and Trevor Immelman to reach the finals.

The great start to the 2007 season saw Stenson move to first on the European Tour and 23rd on the PGA Tour money list; it also gave every reason to believe that the golfer called "Iceman," whose career was once as dead as his nickname suggested, had come back to life and was truly a golfer with ice in his veins — an unflappable golfer. ■

LEE *WESTWOOD*

Born: Worksop, England, April 24, 1973

Perhaps Lee Westwood should be called the British Tiger. While Woods was having the greatest year in golf history in 2000 on the PGA Tour, Westwood was having an almost equally brilliant summer on the European Tour, setting records that might never be broken and establishing himself as the finest golfer on the continent.

Westwood finished sixth on the Order of Merit in 1996, moved up to third for the next three years, and finally became the number one in 2000 after winning six tournaments, a number matched only by Colin Montgomerie, Seve Ballesteros and Nick Faldo. He earned more than £3 million (more than $6 million) and had eight other top-10 finishes. Incredibly, the only cut he missed all year — Europe and the U.S. combined — was at the Masters in Augusta, Georgia.

It was only at age 13 that Westwood started to play golf, yet this game, which takes years to master, came to him almost easily. By the time he was 20, he had turned pro and was competing throughout Europe with the world's best players outside the PGA Tour. His first great success was a win at the Scandinavian Masters in 1996, and a year later he won the prestigious, season-ending Volvo Masters.

That 1997 season also saw him make his first foray into the U.S. where he played seven times, making every cut and finishing no worse than

29th. He rose to even greater prominence in 1998. That year, Westwood won four times in Europe as well as taking the Freeport-McDermott Classic, his first PGA Tour win. He won three times the next year in Europe, and produced two great results early in the season on the PGA Tour. In late March 1999, he finished in a tie for sixth at the Players Championship, and two weeks later had the same finish at the Masters.

While he was tearing apart the European Tour in 2000, Westwood enjoyed great success in the U.S. as well. He finished second at the season-ending American Express Championship and missed only one cut in nine events.

Although he hasn't won in the U.S. since 1998, and hasn't been able to replicate his miracle year of 2000 in Europe, Westwood is really a European golfer who visits the U.S. rather than a true PGA Tour pro. He has consistently made his reputation as a match-play golfer, notably at the Ryder Cup.

CAREER *HIGHLIGHTS*

Turned Pro: 1993

PGA Wins: 1

First PGA Win: 1998

Best Season-end Placing: 130th (2006)

Ryder Cup: 5

Presidents Cup: n/a

In 2004, Westwood earned 4½ points for the Europeans, winning four times and halving his other match. He teamed magnificently with Clarke and Sergio Garcia before beating Kenny Perry 1-up on the final day of another dominating win by the Euros.

His crowning glory came in 2006 when he won three matches and halved the only other two he played. His perfect record led the Europeans to a crushing win over the Americans, 18½ points to 9½ points. Westwood teamed with Darren Clarke and Colin Montgomerie in the fourball and foursomes, and in the final day of singles, he beat Chris DiMarco 2-up to add salt to the Americans' wounds on this Sunday. His 3–0–2 record in 2006 improved his career record at the Ryder Cup to 14–8–3, one of the best records in recent times.

He also played four times at the Alfred Dunhill Cup, a stroke- and match-play format at the Old Course of St. Andrews, and three times at the Seve Trophy tournament, winning twice (2002, 2003). The last is another match-play event, pitting a team made up of players from Continental Europe against a team made up of golfers from Great Britain and Ireland. It is named after Spanish great Severiano (Seve) Ballesteros.

Westwood is still in the prime of his career, and although his life is rooted in the European game, he will no doubt win again in the U.S., he is simply too good not to. Yet he is content to make his name in Europe and establish his legacy there as well, so winning on the PGA is not so much a priority to him as it is a bonus. For that European golf fans should be grateful. ∎

LAST CHANCE
FOR GLORY

6

Because time exacts a toll on all players, there is a group of golfers who are past their prime, but still feel competitive enough to try to remain successful on the Tour. These Last Chance for Glory players may feel the lure of the Champions Tour as they approach the age of 50, or they may feel the pressure of being challenged by younger and stronger golfers, but make no mistake — they will not go quietly into the good night without one last push for success.

Top (L-R): Joey Sindelar, Lee Janzen, Fred Funk, Mark Calcavecchia
Bottom: Mark O'Meara

MARK CALCAVECCHIA

Born: Laurel, Nebraska, June 12, 1960

Not many golfers who won a PGA Tour event in 2007 can boast that their first tour win came in 1986. Mark Calcavecchia can, though. He won the PODS Championship at Innisbrook Resort's Copperhead course in March 2007 at the not so tender age of 46, some 21 years after winning the Southwest Golf Classic in 1986. In between, he had some dozen other tour victories, including the 1989 British Open and the 2005 Canadian Open.

As a kid, Calcavecchia was obsessed with bowling because his father ran a bowling alley, and to this day it is one of his favorite distractions away from the golf course. But when his family moved from Nebraska to Florida, he took up golf with a vengeance and developed into one of the U.S.'s bright young stars in the late 1970s. He turned pro in 1981 and for four years had trouble keeping his Tour card. He would go to Q-school, qualify, and then finish well out of the top 125 for automatic qualifying. But in 1986, his win at the Southwest propelled him to 58th on the money list and full-time status for 1987. He hasn't looked back, although recently there have been a couple of close calls.

Calcavecchia made a huge leap from '86 to '87, going from 58th on the money list to 10th, thanks not to any one week, but a consistently high level of play throughout the year. True, he won the

Honda Classic in 1987, but he also had nine top-10 finishes in 26 starts, finishing with more than $500,000 in winnings (a very impressive sum two decades ago).

The four-year period, from 1987 to 1990, was the finest of Calcavecchia's career. He won six times and was a top-10 money earner in each of those years. In 1988, he lost the Masters to Sandy Lyle by a single shot, and won the Australian Open in a rare foray outside the U.S.

The year after (1989), he won his only major, the British Open, in extra holes. He beat Wayne

CAREER HIGHLIGHTS

Turned Pro: 1981

PGA Wins: 13 (1 major)

First PGA Win: 1986

Best Season-end Placing: 5th (1989)

Ryder Cup: 4

Presidents Cup: 1

Grady and Greg Norman in a four-hole playoff at Royal Troon, Scotland, in a year that saw him win three times and finish a career-best fifth on the money list. He also won the Phoenix Open and Nissan Open. But after 1989, the wins started to trickle instead of flow, and his world ranking steadily declined, in part because he was slowed by injuries to his knee and back, his ankle, sleep apnea, and a myriad of golf hurts that, added together, made him feel about a hundred years old.

In 2001, he finally made a critical change by going to a "claw" grip on his putter. The difference was instant and impressive and rejuvenated his career. He won his next significant tournament in 2005 at the Shaughnessy Golf and Country Club in Vancouver, claiming the Canadian Open by one stroke over Ben Crane and Ryan Moore. He won by leading after every round and, at 45, became the oldest winner in the history of the "fifth major."

Just to show he wasn't going into the good night of the Champions Tour quietly, Calcavecchia racked up an impressive 2007 showing. He won the PODS Championship in strange fashion on the final hole. After carding an incredible 62 on Saturday to put himself in position to win, he had a two-stroke lead on the 72nd hole over playing partner Heath Slocum. Calcavecchia missed his putt for par and Slocum examined his own 4-foot putt for birdie to get a tie and force a playoff. It was, as they say, a gimme. But Slocum missed. Calcavecchia won. The old man still had a few good rounds of golf left in his swing. ∎

FRED *FUNK*

Born: Tacoma Park, Maryland, June 14, 1956

One of the more popular players on tour, Funk is known for his long smile, short drives, and career-long consistency as a player. Perhaps most remarkable of all, though, is that after graduating from the University of Maryland in 1980, and turning pro the next year, he didn't start playing on the PGA Tour full-time until 1989.

For nearly every other golfer, that eight-year gap would have been filled by playing events in Europe or the Nationwide Tour, qualifying tournaments and the like, but Funk immediately took his pro status and became a coach at his alma mater, the University of Maryland. He played a couple of PGA events a year during his time as coach, but it was several years before he decided to take a golf career seriously. Finally, in 1989, he played 29 events and devoted all his time and energy to the tour.

To get to the PGA that season (1989), Funk had qualified through Q-school the previous winter, but at the end of his rookie year he was right back to where he started, after finishing a distant 157th on the money list. That was nearly two decades ago, and it was the last time he had to qualify.

Right from the get-go, Funk earned a reputation for his driving. Not a big man, or a powerful one, or someone who relies on technology for distance,

he has never been a long-ball hitter, but he was always very accurate off the tee. Indeed, he has led the PGA in driving accuracy in seven of the last 14 years. Yet for all the worth of an accurate tee shot, the power hitters have consistently proved that length is far more important than placement, and strength more important than fairway position. In other words, it's more favorable to hit a 9-iron from the rough than a 7-iron from the fairway.

Funk won his first tournament in 1992, the Houston Open, after shooting a 62 on Saturday and holding off Kirk Triplett on the final day for a two-stroke win. He didn't win again for three years. In 1995, though, he won twice and won again the following year as well, the best stretch of golf during his career. In all, he has won eight times on tour, no victory more cherished, though, than his win at the Players Championship in 2005.

CAREER *HIGHLIGHTS*

Turned Pro: 1981

PGA Wins: 8

First PGA Win: 1992

Best Season-end Placing: 11th (2005)

Ryder Cup: 1

Presidents Cup: 2

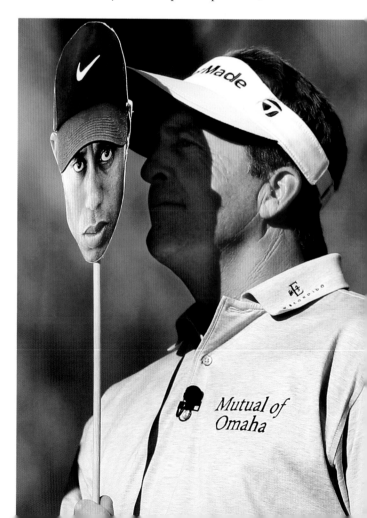

Of course, anyone who wins the prestigious Players tournament has made his mark on the game's history, but Funk did so in a particularly fine fashion. Poor weather forced delays and cancellations such that Funk had to play 33 holes on Monday to finish 72 holes. He ended at 9-under par after a great up-and-down from off the green on the 18th hole, and then watched as Luke Donald and Joe Durant played the final hole with a chance to tie him. Neither player made the necessary birdie, and so, in 2005, at 48 years of age, Funk became the oldest winner of the tournament in nearly half a century. And he did it by outlasting players half his age on a grueling final day.

The win not only gave him a five-year exemption on the PGA Tour, extending past age 50, at which time he will qualify for the Champions Tour, it also earned him a place on the American side for the Presidents Cup, the second appearance of his career. (He also played previously at the Ryder Cup in 2004.) Unfortunately, his record at the 2005 Presidents Cup was a disappointing 0–2–2.

For all of Funk's longevity and solid golf game and accuracy off the tee, his performance in the four majors has been strangely horrible. He hasn't played the British Open for much of his career, and in the six times he did play, he missed the cut three times, and withdrew once. He finished 73rd in 1992 and tied for 66th in 2006. He has played the Masters only 12 times, missing the cut eight times. His best finish was a tie for 17th in 1997. He has played 19 U.S. Opens, missing eight cuts and having a career-best finish of sixth place in 2004. His tie for fourth place at the PGA Championship in 2002 has been by far his best result. ■

LEE JANZEN

Born: Austin, Minnesota, August 28, 1964

Despite enormous promise as a teen, Lee Janzen always felt a hollowness in his life when that life consisted only of golf. He grew up a believer in God, and as he got older and more successful, that belief grew stronger. On the course, he was one of the best there was in the mid-1990s, but off the course it took him many years to find peace with himself. In fact, as a teen, Janzen led what seemed like a double life. He golfed almost all the time and won his first tournament at age 15, by which time he was a scratch golfer. On the other hand, he was also spending time in church, through the influence of his brother who was a youth minister.

Janzen's life changed profoundly at 16 just as he was developing into one of the best junior golfers in the U.S. He was badly hurt in a car accident and doctors had to remove an artery in his right ankle to put in his right arm. Recovery was slow but complete, and he thanked God for his ability to return to the golf course.

Janzen had dreamed of going to a top college on full scholarship, but that dream was modified because of the injury. Instead, he attended Florida Southern College where he was a good golfer, but a poor student. He qualified for the 1985 U.S. Open as an amateur and won the 1986 national championship in Division II while at FSC. Janzen turned pro later in 1986 and played wherever he could get an invitation or exemption or qualify to play. He led the U.S. Golf Tour in winnings in 1989, and after several years on min-tours and at Q-school, he made the PGA Tour full-time in 1991. He won his first tournament the year after (the Northern Telecom Open) by shooting a final-round 65, but his first sensational moment came the next year.

Playing at Baltusrol at the 1993 U.S. Open, Janzen tied the tournament record of 272 to defeat Payne Stewart by two strokes. Amazingly, five years later in 1998, at the Olympic Club in San Francisco, Janzen bettered Stewart again. That year, Stewart led the U.S. Open by five strokes after 54 holes, but Janzen roared back with a 68 on Sunday to defeat Stewart by a single stroke for his second major title.

In 1995, Janzen had his best year, winning three times and finishing third on the money list. He won the Kemper Open in thrilling fashion, scoring a birdie on the final hole to tie Corey Pavin and force a playoff; and then making birdie on the

CAREER HIGHLIGHTS

Turned Pro: 1986

PGA Wins: 8 (2 majors)

First PGA Win: 1992

Best Season-end Placing: 3rd (1995)

Ryder Cup: 2

Presidents Cup: 1

18th again — the first playoff hole — to earn the victory. Janzen also won the Players Championship and Sprint International that year.

More recently, however, Janzen's career has gone south. He hasn't won since the '98 U.S. Open and now plays primarily through exemptions related to his major victories or his seniority. Indeed, his best U.S. Open finish since then was a tie for 13th in 2007, a great result after tying for 80th in 2002

and missing the cut or not qualifying for virtually every major since 1998.

Janzen made the cut in just six of his first 15 tournaments in 2007, but he continues to speak about his beliefs and is a contented man. He may be a two-time major winner, but having a great family and a love for God is clearly something that means more to him than any putt for birdie on the 72nd hole. ∎

Although he has passed the big five-o and is now more associated with fly-fishing or the Champions (i.e., Seniors) Tour than the PGA Tour, Mark O'Meara can die a happy man — for several reasons. In more than a quarter century of golf, he has won some 30 tournaments worldwide. He has represented his country in the Ryder Cup and Presidents Cup. And, in 1998, he had what must have seemed like an out-of-body experience, becoming the oldest man in golf history to win two majors in a season. The 41-year-old captured the Masters and British Open en route to Player of the Year honors, some 18 years after turning pro. He capped that season by beating his close friend, Tiger Woods, in the World Match Play Championship at Wentworth.

The Masters Tournament in 1998 was something to remember for O'Meara. He had never won a major in 56 previous tries, but this time he started with rounds of 74 and 70, decent enough, but not anything spectacular. On Saturday, he shot a 68 and put himself in contention, sitting two behind leader Fred Couples. And then, during the final round on Sunday, he started to sense the possibilities. O'Meara narrowly missed a birdie on the 16th hole, and then made two great drives and approaches on the 17th and 18th. He made both birdie putts and won the green jacket by one shot over Couples and David Duval. After signing his scorecard, he headed to Butler Cabin for the presentation. There stood the 1997 champion, his close friend, neighbor in Orlando and world number one, Tiger Woods, ready to help him into the champion's jacket. This was a dream O'Meara could not have dared to dream. It was his 15th Masters appearance. No golfer had ever played so often before winning for the first time.

A few months later, at the British Open,

O'Meara continued to play with a magic he had never before possessed. He had birdied four holes on the back nine of the brutally tough Royal Birkdale to fend off the charging Tiger Woods, and when Brian Watts played a remarkable bunker shot at the final hole which landed beside the cup for a par, a playoff was forced. O'Meara thrived under the pressure of the four-hole playoff as Watts crumbled — missing great birdie chances on the first two playoff holes, the 15th and 16th, while O'Meara birdied the 15th and made par the rest of the way. He won by two strokes to add a claret jug to his green jacket.

O'Meara capped off 1998 with an astounding win at the World Match Play Championship in England. In the semifinals, he destroyed Vijay Singh 11-and-10, the worst beating in the history of that event. Then, in the finals, he holed his putt from off the green on the 18th to defeat Tiger Woods 1-up. He could not have scripted a better season.

O'Meara won his first tournament in 1984, the Greater Milwaukee Open, and his last PGA tour win remains the British Open in 1998 (although he won the Dubai Classic in 2004). In all, he has won 16 tournaments on the PGA, but he has been as famous for playing golf around the world as he has been for playing at home in the U.S. He enjoyed walking courses abroad, and

he won on every continent except Antarctica. Yet that magical 1998 season was pretty much his last hurrah. His performance declined and his ranking slipped and, as he neared 50, he was drawing more pleasure from fly-fishing than anticipating more golf on the Champions Tour.

In the 21st century, O'Meara is well known for being Tiger's friend and frequent practice partner, but his interests and competitive balance no longer lie in PGA wins. Golf has made him a very rich man, and now he is doing what he wants to do in life. That means a little golf — as a Veteran Member on the PGA in 2007 — and plenty of fishing and traveling with his family. O'Meara's days of pressure golf are over, but he remains a part of golf's recent history, thanks to those few magical months in 1998. ∎

CAREER *HIGHLIGHTS*

Turned Pro: 1980

PGA Wins: 16 (2 majors)

First PGA Win: 1984

Best Season-end Placing: 2nd (1984)

Ryder Cup: 5

Presidents Cup: 2

JOEY SINDELAR

Born: Fort Knox, Kentucky, March 30, 1958

As Joey Sindelar prepares himself for a career on the over-50 Champions Tour, he can look back at a PGA career that has taken him all over the world, written him checks to the tune of more than $11 million and made him a lucky and happy man. His dad delivered mail for 35 years and his mom drove a school bus, a reality which has no doubt given Sindelar a further appreciation of how far he's made it and how fortunate he is.

Although he was born in Kentucky, Sindelar grew up in New York State, where he won just about every amateur golf tournament possible. At age 14, he won the New York State Junior Championship, and he continued to win the more senior amateur titles as he got older. At Ohio State University, he led the golf team to the 1979 NCAA title. In all, he won 10 tournaments while at Ohio before graduating in 1981, at which time he turned pro and made his way to the PGA, looking for fame and fortune.

Sindelar had a tough couple of years at the start of his pro career, but by 1984 he was playing full-time on the PGA Tour. In his first season he made the cut in 23 of 33 tournaments, had three top-10 finishes and ended the year in 59th place on the money list. In 1985 he fared even better, winning two tournaments and ending up 12th on the money list. His first win came at the Greater Greensboro Open, followed by a one-stroke win over Mike Reid at the B.C. Open.

It is 1988 that Sindelar can look back on as the highlight of his career. He finished third on the money list, thanks to an amazing ten top-10 finishes in 30 events. These included wins at the Honda Classic and The International, as well as two runner-up finishes and a third place in another event.

His sixth career win came at the Hardee's Golf Classic in 1990, and thereafter followed a drought

of near epic proportions. Year after year passed as Sindelar played his usual 25 to 30 tournaments, but with nary a victory — until 2004, that is. Coming into the Wachovia Championship at Quail Hollow Club in Charlotte, North Carolina, Sindelar was ranked 222nd and had not won

in his previous 370 starts. There was no reason whatsoever to think it would not be 371 without a victory by the end of the week, except that, for whatever reason, he scored well against the field.

After three solid rounds of 69–69–70, he was in the thick of things with Aaron Oberholser. On Sunday, Sindelar made birdie at the 15th, 16th, and 17th holes before making par at the final to close at 11-under. Oberholser was two strokes ahead with three holes to play, but bogeyed the 16th and 17th and holed a superb up-and-down at the 18th to force the playoff.

Both players made par on the 18th again, the first extra hole, but on the 16th, the second playoff hole, Sindelar made his par and Oberholser bogeyed after hooking his drive into a bunker. The 46-year-old became the oldest Tour winner of 2004 with his unexpected victory. Only Ed Fiori, who went 409 starts between wins, had had a longer drought. Incredibly, Sindelar's check for

$1,008,000 was larger than any other year's worth of winnings he had accrued in 20 years on tour.

Unfortunately, Sindelar has started another streak. Wachovia in 2004 represents his most recent victory, and he has now gone more than 60 events without winning again. There may be a few more Sunday battles left in Sindelar, and fortunately for him, the Champions Tour is much closer than Fiori's 409 record. ∎

CAREER *HIGHLIGHTS*

Turned Pro: 1981

PGA Wins: 7

First PGA Win: 1985

Best Season-end Placing: 3rd (1988)

Ryder Cup: 0

Presidents Cup: 0

QUEENS
OF CLUBS

7

No area of golf has improved and grown worldwide to the extent the women's game has. From the enormous success of several Asian players, to an emerging rivalry between Annika Sorenstam and Lorena Ochoa, to the maturity of great young women like Paula Creamer and Natalie Gulbis, the LPGA has seen a remarkable increase in its television audience and tournament crowds. Today's female golfers have their own fan followings within the galleries, and as the competition for the top spots gets tougher and tougher, the future of the women's game gets more and more exciting.

Top (L-R): Se Ri Pak, Annika Sorenstam, Natalie Gulbis, Morgan Pressel
Bottom: Lorena Ochoa

PAULA *CREAMER*

Born: Mountain View, California, August 5, 1986

They call her the Pink Panther, and if there is a golf equivalent to the ambitious and chic character Reese Witherspoon plays in the *Legally Blonde* movies, it's the preppy, perky professional from California who wears pink 24/7. But cute as her pink-themed image is, though, it was Paula Creamer's breakout season in 2007 that made her one of the top golfers in the game today.

The swift and dramatic rise of Creamer to the top of her profession has come as a result of years of playing and practicing. Creamer is a superb player who won some 19 amateur titles in the U.S. before turning pro in 2005. She is also one of a group of young golfers who are both talented and fitness-oriented, marking a new wave in the women's game that has fans flocking to the course like never before.

Creamer was a semifinalist in the U.S. Women's Amateur Championship in both 2003 and 2004 and, at the end of the latter year, she won the qualifying tournament by five strokes to earn her LPGA Tour card for 2005. She immediately announced her intentions of turning pro, and planned for a career in golf at age 18.

Her rookie season only added to her reputation. Creamer won her first LPGA tournament in May 2005 when she finished first at the Sybase Classic, the youngest winner of a multi-round LPGA event in Tour history. Four days later, she graduated from high school. Creamer later won

events in France and Japan and earned a spot on the Solheim Cup team for the U.S., the youngest player ever to do so, and the only rookie ever to make the team. To prove this was no fluke, she earned 3.5 points for the victorious side, including

CAREER *HIGHLIGHTS*

Turned Pro: 2005

LPGA Wins: 3

First LPGA Win: 2005

Best Season-end Placing: 2nd (2005)

Solheim Cup: 2

a crushing 7-and-5 win over Laura Davies, one of the greats from a previous generation, in the singles matches on the final day. Creamer made more than $1.5 million, finished second in LPGA earnings, and was named Rookie of the Year. Only Annika Sorenstam earned more money that year.

Although she failed to win in 2006, Creamer nonetheless played highly respectable golf. She finished in the top 10 some 14 times and ranked 11th in yearly earnings, becoming the first player to pass $1 million for a year in which she didn't win. In all, she missed only two cuts in the first 62 events she entered.

Creamer bounced back early in 2007, winning the first event of the year, the SBS Open in Kahuku, Hawaii. She continued her strong play throughout the summer, finishing 4th, 2nd, 4th and 6th in one stretch. In all, Creamer finished in the top 10 in more than half her tournaments (12 of 22 events), earning well over $1 million for the third straight year, and finishing in the top five of the money list again. Incredibly, she missed only four cuts in 84 career tournaments through the end of the 2007 season, a testament to her consistency and focus on the course.

Her ascent to the first class of women's golfers was solidified late in 2007 through two events. She was named to the Solheim Cup team for the second time, and she went undefeated in five matches, leading the U.S. women to a convincing 16–12 win over the European team at the Halstad Golf Club in Halmstad, Sweden. In the foursomes, she and veteran Juli Inkster defeated Laura Davies and Becky Brewerton 2-and-1, and in the afternoon fourball, she and equally youthful Morgan Pressel halved with Davies and Trish Johnson. On the second day, she teamed with Inkster and Brittany Lincicome to halve two more matches, and in the singles on the final day, Creamer beat Maria Hjorth 2-and-1 to complete her undefeated weekend and solidify her reputation as one of the best young players in the world.

Then, in early November, she won the exclusive Tournament of Champions in dominating style, winning by eight strokes over Birdie Kim, the

nearest competitor. True to her self-image, she said the win was doubly satisfying because she won playing with a pink ball.

In truth, Creamer might be the next golfer to challenge Lorena Ochoa for the number-one ranking. She hits the ball straight as an arrow, has superb control of her irons and is one of the best clutch putters on tour. She has everything it takes to win, except maybe experience. With her ambition, that, of course, will develop every day, every tournament. ∎

NATALIE *GULBIS*

Born: Sacramento, California, January 7, 1983

In sports, where gaining respect is harder for women than for men, and where the body is more overtly the focus than the sport, Natalie Gulbis occupies a unique niche: a talented golfer who is admired both for her swing and her sex appeal. For the longest time she was considered a mere pin-up girl with no substance, marketing her image while her golf game faded into the background. Then she won the LPGA 2007 Evian Masters in a playoff, and golf game challenged image for ultimate recognition.

Gulbis won the 1997 California Women's Amateur Championship at age 14, and a short time later qualified for the Longs Drugs Challenge, an LPGA event. At the time she was the youngest player to qualify on the Monday of a tournament in LPGA history. She played on her high school's boys' team, but not for long. She graduated from grade 12 at age 16 and went on to play one season of college golf while at the University of Arizona, winning four times and qualifying for the U.S. Women's Open as an amateur. She turned pro in 2001 at the age of 18.

The same year she turned pro, Gulbis earned her LPGA card for the next year by finishing third at Q-school and, as an LPGA rookie in 2002, she played 26 events. In a world where teen phenoms catapult to the top overnight, and stars are made so early in life, it's difficult to modify expectations or consider the possibility that a young star might actually be a late bloomer.

She had her share of solid rounds and finished in the top 20 of the majors for nine consecutive tournaments between 2004 and 2006, but Gulbis caused quite a stir prior to the 2004 U.S. Women's Open. At that time, she produced a full-color wall calendar for 2005 showing her in provocative positions and wearing sometimes skimpy, tight-fitting clothing and swimsuits. The USGA barred its sale at tournaments, citing it as inappropriate, but LPGA commissioner Ty Votaw was not only happy with Gulbis's calendar, he was happy for the attention it brought the game. She has since posed for men's magazines, while still producing her own calendar and starting her own reality television show in 2006: all of which have added to her appeal away from the golf course.

In 2005, Gulbis finished sixth in earnings on the LPGA Tour with more than $1 million, and in 2007, she earned her first victory under dramatic circumstances. She was four strokes back to start the final round of the Evian Masters in Evian-

CAREER *HIGHLIGHTS*

Turned Pro: 2001

LPGA Wins: 1

First LPGA Win: 2007

Best Season-end Placing: 6th (2005)

Solheim Cup: 1

les-Bains, France, but shot a 70 to gain a tie with Jeong Jang at – 4 after 72 holes. On the first playoff hole, Gulbis birdied the par-5 hole and Jang could manage only a par. This time, the photo-op was as a result of her swing, not her smile.

She played only infrequently during the last half of 2007, finishing in a tie for fourth at the Longs Drugs Challenge in October. Her crowning glory, though, took place a month earlier, at the Solheim Cup in Sweden. Although she lost in the foursomes and fourball matches, Gulbis won her singles match on the final day, a sound 4-and-3 win over Gwaldys Nocera to help the Americans defeat Europe 16–12. It was an important competition for her development as a player, and should give her added confidence as her career moves forward, a career certain to garner plenty of attention for both her image and her game. ∎

In a seeming flash, Lorena Ochoa burst onto the golf scene to become the number-one woman golfer in the world, making Annika Sorenstam disappear as if by magic. That flash occurred in the fall of 2006, a mere three seasons after Ochoa had joined the LPGA as a pro.

Ochoa made the LPGA Tour by virtue of finishing first in the Futures Tour in 2002, and since joining the LPGA in '03, her rise has been meteoric and unstoppable. It could hardly have been a surprise, however. Ochoa had one of the greatest amateur careers of all time. In just two years at the University of Arizona, she won 12 collegiate tournaments, including a record eight in a row. She was the NCAA Player of the Year in 2001–02, and her career totals in university are staggering: 20 tournaments entered, 12 victories,

six runner-up finishes. In the events she didn't win, she never lost by more than three strokes.

Ochoa turned pro in May 2002, halfway through her university program and was an instant success on the Futures Tour, winning three times in the summer and finishing first on the money list. Her first year on the LPGA Tour was another success, and her eight top-10 finishes were enough to earn her Rookie of the Year. Still, this was just the beginning.

In 2004, Ochoa won her first two tournaments, the Franklin American Mortgage Championship and the LPGA Classic, thus becoming the first Mexican-born player to win on the LPGA Tour. She also finished in the top 10 in three of the four major championships — tied for eighth at the Kraft Nabisco Championship and

CAREER *HIGHLIGHTS*

Turned Pro: 2002
LPGA Wins: 16 (1 major)
First LPGA Win: 2004
Best Season-end Placing: 1st (2007)
Solheim Cup: n/a

the LPGA Championship and fourth at the Women's British Open. She finished 44th at the U.S. Women's Open. The next year she won the Wegmans Rochester LPGA event and finished runner-up four other times, including a playoff loss to the number-one golfer in the world, the aforementioned Annika Sorenstam.

In 2006, Ochoa completed her ascent and became the top women's golfer on the planet. She shot a 62 in the first round of the LPGA Kraft Nabisco Championship, the lowest score ever in the majors by a man or woman, and she went on to finish second after losing a playoff to Karrie Webb. Nonetheless, Ochoa won six tournaments that year and finished second on six other occasions. In 25 tournaments, she made the cut every time and finished in the top 10 an amazing 20 times.

She led the Tour in winnings during 2006, but it was in October of that year that she made her biggest statement, both psychologically and sportingly. This came at the Samsung World Championship, an exclusive, invitation-only tournament with a limited field of 20. To start the final round, Ochoa was three strokes behind Sorenstam, and the two were paired in the final grouping. Ochoa went out and shot a 65, while Sorenstam managed only a 70. The win was the biggest of Ochoa's career until 2007 when she established herself as the clear number-one golfer.

In 2007, Ochoa did what she had so narrowly failed to do the previous year — win her first major championship. In the summer, the LPGA played the Women's British Open at the Old Course at St. Andrews, the first professional tournament for women ever held on golf's sacred

— but male-dominated — land. Ochoa took the lead on the ninth hole on the first day of play and never looked back, winning by four strokes and posing with the trophy at the famous Swilcan Bridge in the 18th fairway. The next week, she won the Canadian Women's Open, and the week after that she captured the Safeway Classic, making her and Sorenstam the only female golfers in the last 25 years to claim three consecutive victories. In all, her amazing 2007 season saw Ochoa win eight times and finish second on six other occasions. Incredibly, she finished in the top 10 in 20 of 23 events she entered.

Ochoa is only 26 years old and already has 16 career wins on the LPGA Tour. There is no limit to what she might accomplish in the next decade and beyond. The possibilities are there for the taking, but 2008 will be more of a challenge as Sorenstam promises a fight for the title of best woman golfer in the world. ■

The only country in the world where women's golf is hands down more popular than the men's game is South Korea, and there is no one golfer who has influenced that shift in popularity more than the legendary Se Ri Pak. Her extraordinary career and accomplishments might be less well-known to the average golf fan only because, for many fans, women's golf starts and finishes with Annika Sorenstam. But Pak has for years been the number-two women's golfer in the world, and in Asia she is revered with god-like admiration.

Pak's story is the stuff of legend. She gave up track and field at age 14 to work on golf, and she trained under her father for years. He had been a gang member, which perhaps accounts for his training methods. His regimen for his teen daughter either verged on child abuse or brilliance for its harsh innovation, depending on how one wants to view the stories.

He made Pak hit golf balls barefoot in the snow. Once, after telling him that she was afraid of cemeteries, he forced her to hit balls and sleep in a cemetery to overcome those fears. She got up at 5:30 every morning and ran up and down the 14 flights of stairs in their apartment building — forwards and backwards. And then there was the golf: some six hours a day, seven days a week, on the range and on the course. She had the body of a track star, and by the time her father had finished with her she was a golfer in better shape than most heptathletes. Her training also made her one of the most relentless and toughest competitors in golf.

The training, combined with her natural talent, paid off, but hers was not a wealthy family. Pak turned pro so that she could play on the Korean Women's Tour, and in only two years and

CAREER *HIGHLIGHTS*

Turned Pro: 1998

LPGA Wins: 24 (5 majors)

First LPGA Win: 1998

Best Season-end Placing: 2nd (1998, 2001–03)

Solheim Cup: n/a

14 tournaments she won six times and finished second seven times. This earned her a lucrative endorsement deal and with it the chance to come to the U.S. to play on the LPGA.

Pak was an instant success. She qualified through Q-school for the LPGA Tour in her first attempt, and as a rookie in 1998 she won four tournaments. The first two tournaments were majors, the LPGA and the U.S. Women's Open, and she won two more in quick succession. She finished second on the money list and was named Rookie of the Year, and this beginning was a mere portent of greater things to come.

In her decade on tour, Pak has failed to win in only two seasons, 2000 and 2005. After 2000, she was so disappointed with her game that she hired a new coach, revamped her swing and vowed to improve. In 2001, she won five times, finished in the top 10 some 12 times, and finished second on

the money list. The year after, her numbers were the same: five wins, second on the money list. Mission accomplished.

In all, Pak has won five majors and 24 LPGA events, most recently at the 2007 Corning Classic when she blew a lead on the last day to Morgan Pressel, but rallied with four holes to play to eke out a tense, three-stroke win. More important, her success, first in South Korea and then in the U.S., signaled the advent of a huge infusion of Asian talent to the LPGA and a commensurate fan interest in the game in that part of the world. Virtually every top female Asian golfer credits Pak for popularizing the game in the Far East and for inspiring her to reach the LPGA. That list of golfers includes Grace Park, Mi Hyun Kim, Jeong Jang, Angela Park, Young Kim and Seon Hwa Lee among many others. Pak is, above all, the leader of the so-called Seoul Sisters. ∎

MORGAN *PRESSEL*

Born: Tampa, Florida, May 23, 1988

It didn't take young Morgan Pressel long to make a name for herself on the LPGA Tour. After turning pro in 2006, Pressel won one of the LPGA's four majors in April 2007 by finishing atop the leaderboard at the Kraft Nabisco Championship, the youngest player ever to win a major. It was a remarkable win for the 18-year-old, and it put her among the top young golfers in the women's game.

Pressel had an unusual childhood but has persevered in large measure because of her Jewish heritage which gave her a strong grounding and basis for her character. Her mother died in 2003 after which Morgan went to live with her grandparents, Herb and Evelyn Krickstein, while two younger siblings remained with their father. Herb was her coach for several years. Herb is a retired physician and the father of Aaron Krickstein, a former world-class tennis player who was once ranked sixth in the world.

Pressel made history in 2001 when she qualified for the U.S. Women's Open at age 12, the youngest ever to do so. During her amateur career, she won 11 titles including the "amateur slam," which consists of five American Junior Golf Association (AJGA) invitational tournaments. In 2005, Pressel's last year as an amateur, she made quite an impression before turning pro. She won the U.S. Women's Amateur Championship with a surprisingly easy 9-and-8 win over Maru Martinez in the finals, and she also finished second at the U.S. Women's Open despite still being an amateur. In fact, she and Birdie Kim were tied in the 72nd fairway, but Kim holed a phenomenal bunker shot from off the green and Pressel made bogey to finish two shots back.

In January 2006, Pressel appealed to the LPGA to turn pro, a required process for anyone under 18. Commissioner Ty Votaw consented, and the 17-year-old started playing full-time later that year, after graduating from high school. The same year she earned her LPGA Tour card by finishing in a tie for sixth at Q-school.

Her rookie season of 2006 was a perfectly respectable, if not spectacular, one. She made 21 of 23 cuts, had nine finishes in the top 10, and earned nearly half a million dollars, good for 24th on the

CAREER *HIGHLIGHTS*

Turned Pro: 2006

LPGA Wins: 1 (1 major)

First LPGA Win: 2007

Best Season-end Placing: 7th (2007)

Solheim Cup: 1

money list. But she really made her mark at the Kraft Nabisco Championship in Rancho Mirage, California, in April 2007. Not among the leaders on the final round, she played in relative obscurity, walking off the 18th hole at –3. She trailed the leaders (who were still on the course when she headed to the clubhouse) by three strokes. But one by one, Catriona Matthew, Brittany Lincicome and Suzann Pettersen all fell by the wayside, and Pressel's score was best by one stroke.

She almost won her second tournament in mid-July at the Owens Corning Classic. She and Se Ri Pak were the final pairing on Sunday, Pressel trailing by two shots. But Pak had troubles early on and Pressel played brilliantly. At the par-3, seventh hole, she scored a hole-in-one to lead by three strokes, but Pak was not to be dissuaded. She nearly holed her fairway shot at the 15th, and the tap-in

birdie gave her a one-shot lead. Pak nearly did the same on the closing hole, but her three-stroke win was much closer than it looked on paper.

Pressel's crowning glory of 2007, however, came at the Solheim Cup in Sweden. As a member of the U.S. team, Pressel lost one match and halved another on the first day, and lost again on the second day. But in the singles matches, she went head-to-head with Annika Sorenstam, a hero in her native Sweden. True, Sorenstam had been recovering from injuries, but Pressel nonetheless went out and defeated the long-time number-one player in the world 2-and-1, an enormous psychological win for the emerging teenager.

Pressel, now 19 years old, has leap-frogged over several other young notable stars to become perhaps the best young player in golf. With her already impressive numbers, the future looks bright. ∎

I t took Annika Sorenstam exactly one year to go from being an LPGA rookie to being the number-one women's golfer in the world. Between 1995 and 2006, she won more tournaments than any other woman in that time and established herself as one of the greatest and most dominant golfers in the game. Despite missing much of 2007 with injuries, she remains the most respected and successful woman on the LPGA Tour.

Sorenstam was a member of Sweden's national team for six years (1987–92) and she also attended the University of Arizona (1990–92) during which time she won seven tournaments. In 1992, she was the world amateur champion and runner-up at the U.S. Women's Amateur Championship. She turned pro in 1993 and qualified for the LPGA Tour the next season, earning Rookie of the Year honors in '94 for a year that included three top-10 finishes.

In 1995, Sorenstam won her first LPGA tournament — the U.S. Women's Open, one of only 14 players to win a major as her first Tour victory, and she later won the Samsung World Championship in a playoff against the legendary Laura Davies. She took home Player of the Year

CAREER *HIGHLIGHTS*

Turned Pro: 1994

LPGA Wins: 69 (10 majors)

First LPGA Win: 1995

Best Season-end Placing: 1st (1995, 1997–98, 2001–05)

Solheim Cup: 7

honors, becoming only the second player, after Hall of Famer Nancy Lopez, to win Rookie of the Year and Player of the Year in successive seasons. In all, she made the cut in all of the 19 tournaments she entered, had 12 top-10 finishes and was number one in yearly earnings. This was only the start.

In the next decade, Sorenstam rightly earned comparisons to Tiger Woods for her skill, personality, and ability to dominate the game. The two great golfers became known for swapping text messages every time each won a major championship, forming a pleasant rivalry and friendship in the process. Sorenstam has won 10 majors to date. Following her 1995 U.S. Women's Open win, she won that event again the next year and again in 2006. She also won three Kraft Nabisco Championships, three LPGA titles, and one British Women's Open. In all, she has won 69 tournaments on the LPGA Tour and has earned more money than anyone in the history of the women's game. She was never ranked lower than fourth from 1995 to 2006 and missed only four cuts in the 250 tournaments she entered.

Sorenstam made headlines in May 2003 when she played a PGA Tour event, the first woman to do so since 1945. She entered the Bank of America Colonial in Fort Worth, Texas, but missed the cut after rounds of 71 and 75. Still, she earned respect among the men for her poise and skill.

After winning 10 tournaments in 2005, Sorenstam won only three in '06 and in 2007 she had the worst year of her career because of a painful and debilitating back injury. She tried to fight the pain early in the year before leaving the Tour altogether to deal with the pain, missing most of the summer and never feeling good about her swing all season. In all, she was able to compete in only 11 events in '07, finishing in the top 10 in five of those, but failing to record a win for the first time in her career. Toward the end of the year, though, she pronounced herself healthy and motivated to return to the number-one ranking in '08, a ranking she has enjoyed much of her life on the LPGA Tour.

In a career filled with firsts and bests, Sorenstam has taken women's golf to new levels of respect and popularity. She has been named Player of the Year an unprecedented eight times and qualified for induction into the Golf Hall of Fame after only seven years on tour. More important, though, her golf game brought women's golf into prime-time television (she played a Skins Game with Tiger Woods, David Duval and Karrie Webb), the front page of the sports news and the nightly TV highlight reels. Sorenstam's domination, which may be over thanks to Lorena Ochoa, gave women's golf its first modern superstar, and for that she will be remembered as much as for any single shot or victory. ■

Quite simply the finest woman golfer Australia has produced, Karrie Webb has been a mainstay atop the leaderboard around the world for more than a decade. She has won more than 40 tournaments, including seven majors on the LPGA Tour, and has earned more than $13 million in a career full of glory.

Webb became the stroke play champion of Australia in 1994, the same year she embarked on a pro career on the Ladies European Tour. The

next year, her first full season as a pro, she became the youngest-ever winner of the Women's British Open and was named Rookie of the Year. At season's end, she qualified for the LPGA through Q-school and has never looked back.

Needing no time at all to become familiar with the greater competition provided by the LPGA, Webb won her first tournament in just her second start, that at the 1996 Healthsouth Inaugural Tournament. She won on the fourth playoff hole, defeating Martha Nause and Jane Geddes. In all that year, she won four times, finished second five times and became the first player in LPGA history to win $1 million in a season. She also finished first in season earnings, and all of this in her rookie season. Of course, she was named Rookie of the Year for 1996.

Webb has had a winless season only twice since 1996, the first in 2005, the second in 2007. She had her finest years in 1999 and 2000, when she won six and seven tournaments, respectively, and finished first in earnings. She won three majors during that stretch as well — the du Maurier Classic and Kraft Nabisco Championship in 1999, and the U.S. Women's Open the following year. In 1999, she set an astounding record by finishing in the top 10 in 16 straight tournaments. By winning the LPGA Championship in 2001, Webb, at 26, became the youngest woman to win the career grand slam.

The year 2001 was also historic for women's golf. Webb teamed with David Duval against Annika Sorenstam and Tiger Woods at a made-for-TV Skins Game at Bighorn, the most-watched golf event involving women ever.

Webb's most dramatic win came in 2006 at the Kraft Nabisco Championship. Standing in the fairway of the 72nd hole, she trailed Lorena Ochoa by two strokes and needed to hole her fairway shot just to tie. She pulled out a wedge,

and from 116 yards did, indeed, hole out to send the tournament to a playoff, much to the shock of Ochoa. Webb needed only one extra hole to win, making a seven-foot putt for birdie, and her victory from seven shots back after three rounds tied the record for the biggest rally in LPGA history. The win was her seventh major and gave her more than $12 million in career earnings, making her only the second golfer after Sorenstam to reach this milestone.

Webb won the Women's British Open twice (1995 and 1997) before it was considered a major, and once after it was given major status (2002). The 2002 win was doubly important because she became the first woman to achieve the Super Grand Slam, winning all five major championships during her career. Further, her sixth major at age 27 made her the second youngest to get to this plateau after the great Mickey Wright.

Webb has also been named Player of the Year twice. Still, she has slumped noticeably in recent years. Despite her fine 2006 season, she went winless in 2005 and again in 2007, although she did finish second at the LPGA Championship in '07 to Suzann Pettersen, the winner by a single stroke. Nonetheless, Webb qualified through a point system to enter the Golf Hall of Fame — which she did in 2005 — and will go down as one of the LPGA's finest golfers and unquestionably the best woman from Down Under to have played the game. ■

CAREER *HIGHLIGHTS*

Turned Pro: 1994

LPGA Wins: 35 (7 majors)

First LPGA Win: 1995

Best Season-end Placing: 1st (1996, 1999–2000)

Solheim Cup: n/a

MICHELLE *WIE*

Born: Honolulu, Hawaii, October 11, 1989

Like a famous child actor who has trouble finding good roles as an adult, Michelle Wie has not moved gracefully from being a 14-year-old teen phenom nicknamed the "Big Wiesie" to a later-aged teen making a splash as a pro in the world of women's golf. Indeed, after 2007, it can fairly be said that a career once deep in promise and future glory is now almost entirely bereft of same, her game mismanaged by her father and those close to her. While Michelle Wie might be a millionaire many times over, her career is more Anna Kournikova than Annika Sorenstam.

The conundrum is simple and unavoidable. Wie has several "youngest to" and "first to" to her credit, but to date she has never won a 72-hole tournament of any kind, at any level. At age 11, she became the youngest girl to qualify for the USGA Amateur Championship and two years later, at age 13, she became the youngest to qualify for an LPGA event, the Takefuji Classic (she missed the cut).

In 2003, she became the youngest player to make an LPGA cut, at the Kraft Nabisco Championship, and soon after she won the U.S. Amateur Public Links tournament at age 14, the youngest player ever to win an adult event. In 2004, she started on the road to both her dream and, possibly, her ruin. She played in the Sony Open, a men's event, and missed the cut by a single stroke. It seemed certain she would one day play on the men's Tour, as she so longed to do. But over the years, as she has played more and more men's events, she has missed the cut by a greater and greater number of strokes.

CAREER *HIGHLIGHTS*

Turned Pro: no full status yet
LPGA Wins: 0
First LPGA Win: 0
Best Season-end Placing: n/a
Solheim Cup: 0

These early moments of glory brought Wie into the spotlight for several reasons. For starters, she was tall, lean and strong for her age, and could hit the ball farther than any woman on the LPGA Tour. Her swing was powerful and smooth, inspiring golfers to nickname her in honor of Ernie Els, the "Big Easy," for his similar swing. In short, her game seemed to have no flaws that time and experience wouldn't cure. Also, she wanted to break down the various barriers the sport has erected, everything from wanting to qualify for the Masters and be the first female to play at Augusta National, to qualifying for the men's U.S. Open. Players on the men's tour supported her or vilified the sponsors' exemptions which got her into tournaments, but the media frenzy was overwhelming and undeniably good for the game.

Still, Wie didn't fulfill her end of the bargain. That is, her game didn't improve rapidly or at all; in truth, it got worse. She had some success on the LPGA Tour in 2005, her first year playing a limited number of events as a pro, but could never play winning golf on a Sunday — the mark of a true player. By 2006, her involvement in men's tournaments seemed no more than a publicity stunt, as she finished last in several events. On the women's tour, she competed but didn't win. Indeed, the leaderboard seemed to recede further and further from view as she got older.

In 2007, at the Sony Open again, Wie was 142nd of 144 golfers after two rounds, some 25 shots behind the leader, and missed the cut. She suffered a wrist injury which kept her out for several months, and when she returned — some say prematurely — her game was in tatters. Missed cuts and withdrawals pockmarked her résumé, and she shot only one round under par during the last half of the year. If 2007 had started out as her breakthrough year, it ended as her *annus horribilis*.

As her 18th birthday approached, Wie vowed to go to Stanford University on scholarship to get an education and work on her golf game (though she could not play on the college team because she was a professional). More than anything, Wie needs stability and calm and time to work on the fundamentals. Her father has been her caddie on and off for several years, and she has never had the same swing coach for any period of time. She may be rich and famous, but if she wants to grow up to be a winning professional golfer, Wie has a long way to go. ■

ON *THE BAG*

8

Caddies are not just the men and women who haul around golfers' clubs. They are friends and advisors and skilled golfers in their own right. Any great golfer will credit his or her caddie as one of the most important aspects of success. A good caddie will not only measure yardage, but will also suggest club selections and give crucial advice on putts. Caddies are with their golfers on the driving range early in the morning for practice rounds, and right on through to the 72nd green, when a tournament is won or lost. And, like golfers, caddies have their own personalities and following.

Top (L-R): Andy Prodger, Steve Williams, Brennan Little, Mike Cowan
Bottom: Jim MacKay

Devoting a career to the game of golf will likely mean meeting some interesting people along the way, but Fluff Cowan has met more than his fair share of glory golfers in his day. On the other hand, it might be argued that he had the best job in the game — and blew it.

Cowan was a decent golfer going nowhere, so he decided to carry the bag for a while. That was 1976. Early on, Cowan was hired by Peter Jacobsen, and the two stayed together for 18 years, during which Jacobsen won six tournaments. In 1996, Jacobsen suffered injuries that kept him off the course for long stretches. It was during this layoff that Cowan got a call from an amateur

"Jim kind of plays his way around a golf course. Jim hits it far enough, and has been very successful in his career, and I feel I'm very fortunate to have a player that I consider to be one of the ten best players in the world."

Fluff Cowan, after being fired by Tiger Woods and picked up by Jim Furyk.

named Tiger Woods, who was about to turn pro. Woods needed a caddy for several tournaments, and Cowan agreed to help, but with the caveat that when Jacobsen got his health back he'd have to leave Woods.

Of course, Cowan never went back. He was just what Tiger needed, a caddy who knew his way around the Tour, knew the courses and greens and yardage, and could take Woods through those initial steps of what was destined to be a remarkable pro career.

He was with Tiger for three years, notably the 1997 Masters, which Woods won by a preposterous 15 strokes. However, Cowan didn't serve his master so much as himself. Woods demanded privacy above all else from his caddy, but Cowan had a loose lip and Woods got fed up with Cowan's love of the spotlight. Tiger fired him, but Cowan didn't remain unemployed for long.

Just a few weeks later, Jim Furyk fired his caddy and hired Cowan. They had their greatest success in 2003 when Furyk won the U.S. Open, and the pair have been together ever since. In the meantime, Furyk has become one of the top golfers in the world. ∎

ERIC *LARSON*

Mark Calcavecchia

He did the crime, paid his time and got his life back on track — thanks to Mark Calcavecchia, a man who could forgive, as well as play golf. Eric Larson is a lucky man, indeed.

Larson was a caddie, working for Ken Green in the early 1990s. In 1994, he met Calcavecchia and the two got along well. Larson went to work with Calcavecchia, the 1989 British Open winner, and life seemed good. The only problem was that unbeknownst to the golfer, Larson was also acting as middleman for friends who sold cocaine and friends who used the drug. As he saw it, he was doing favors for two sets of friends for a little money on the side. He neither sold it nor used it, so he felt he wasn't doing anything too wrong.

He was finally caught — courtesy of the supplier — and on August 9, 1995, Larson started a 13-year prison sentence. Calcavecchia promised him a job when he got out, and Larson never forgot that act of kindness. Calcavecchia, Green, and other golfers and caddies even kept in touch with Larson during his incarceration. After 10 years in prison (during which he earned a degree in business management), he was released to a halfway house, and another year later he was free to go.

Calcavecchia, meanwhile, had used several caddies in the interim, mostly his ever-reliable wife, Brenda, who perhaps didn't have the qualifications of a caddy in terms of golf knowledge but certainly knew the golfer better than most caddies know their bosses. When Larson was freed, Calcavecchia was true to his word, rehired Larson, and the two resumed their relationship. Larson returned to the bag contrite, knowing every day he was free to do what he wanted was a day extra out of life.

Before being sentenced, he wrote a letter to the judge acknowledging his crime, admitting it was wrong, and promising never to commit a crime again. It might have been a facile communication,

"It shows how much of a friend Mark has been to stay with me. My life is getting back in order. Everything I've worked hard on to get back in this position has paid off."

Eric Larson, soon after being released from prison and rehired by Mark Calcavecchia.

but to Larson it was the genuine article. Later, when he was free and happy, and walking the course with his old buddy Calcavecchia again, he promised to keep that vow. He wasn't going to blow it again. ∎

BRENNAN *LITTLE*

Mike Weir

As is the case in so many situations, timing was everything for Brennan Little and Mike Weir. Together now since 1999, Little has been on the bag for all of Weir's wins, notably the 2003 Masters when Weir became the first Canadian to win the green jacket and the first lefty to win at Augusta, Georgia.

Weir's first caddie was his wife, Bricia, who performed the duties out of necessity, not love of the game. The couple was dirt poor and Weir was struggling, but in 1997 she "retired" and Weir got a friend, Dan Keough, to help. Two years later, though, Keough decided to open a business in Toronto, and that left Weir without a caddy.

Enter Little. The two were the same age and had competed against each other in southern Ontario at various tournaments as teens, but while Mike's

game improved, Little's hadn't. Weir went on to the PGA, but Little struggled on the Canadian Tour. Mike suggested a trial run on the bag to start the 1999 PGA season on the west coast, and Little accepted the job, figuring he'd return to his own career in the summer.

Weir played well during that stretch, though, and Little discovered he had more fun than he had expected. They have been together ever since. Like a good caddy, Little knows when to talk to his golfer to keep him calm, and when to keep quiet to keep him focused.

In the case of this golfer and caddie, though, they have become good friends off the course as well, which is not surprising given the time they spent together during childhood. They have become good friends with several NHL players, notably Adam Oates, as a result of their mutual passion for hockey, and more recently they have appeared in TV ads as well.

Weir won the 2003 Masters with Little on the bag, and they are a perfect pairing, the two Canadians taking on the rest of the world every week on the PGA Tour. ∎

"I've had Brennan helping me out reading greens…I made it a point last week to ask him to help me read greens a little better because I felt like maybe that was what was missing…He's been right on."

Mike Weir, September 2007, discussing his improved play.

JIM *"BONES"* MacKAY

Phil Mickelson

"Bones has been with me from Day One. He's ridden the waves with me, and there's been a lot of waves crashing on us in final rounds. To be riding on the top of the wave this time was really cool."

Mickelson after his 2004 Masters victory.

The lives and careers of Jim MacKay and Phil Mickelson are so similar they almost graft perfectly onto one another. MacKay started caddying in 1990 for Larry Mize after the two met at university, but as soon as Mickelson turned pro in 1993, MacKay joined him. The two have been together ever since. "Together" for these two means never playing a round without the other in 14 years and counting! In fact, MacKay is currently golf's longest-serving caddy for the same player.

MacKay is almost like a playing partner for Mickelson. He is able to give advice from the other side, as it were, because Mickelson is one of the few left-handed players on tour while MacKay is right-handed. MacKay is one of the most vocal caddies for his golfer and offers Mickelson advice on nearly every putt. The most common scenario on any given green is to see Mickelson line up a putt and then MacKay stand over the ball from the other side to judge the line as he sees it. The two then compare notes, and Mickelson makes his putt.

This collaboration is all the more important in Florida, which is MacKay's home turf. Mickelson is from the west, where greens are usually made of Bermuda grass, something that is rare in Florida, so MacKay's advice is precious.

The reserved MacKay got the nickname "Bones" early in his career, when Fred Couples couldn't remember the caddie's name and simply referred to him as Bones. Bones was a golfer at Columbus College in his own right before turning to caddying, and as a result he has no problem offering his own, educated opinion about club selection or course management to Mickelson. Although he gives plenty of advice to his golfer, it is sometimes wrong. This is also part of the caddie-golfer relationship. Like a marriage, they must work through tough times as well as revel in the good times.

In all, the good times have prevailed overwhelmingly. Although it took Mickelson a decade to win a major, he has two Masters titles and one PGA championship to his credit among more than 30 wins around the world. MacKay has been there every step of the way and might have the most secure job in a game that is all about insecurity. ∎

"Though we won two majors [Prodger and Nick Faldo], the most satisfying job was in a loss in a U.S. Open in Brookline, when we lost to Curtis Strange in a playoff. If [Faldo] was making his ten-footers, he would have won very easily, but he didn't."

Andy Prodger, currently caddy for K.J. Choi, reflecting on his years with the legendary Nick Faldo.

In a career that has spanned nearly 30 years on the bag, Andy Prodger has caddied for some of the finest golfers in the game and has won more tournaments than most golfers on tour.

Like many a caddie, Prodger had ambitions to play pro, but he was simply not quite good enough. A scratch golfer, he was an assistant pro at the Hartsfeld Country Club in Watford, England, in the early 1970s, but being a scratch golfer and being able to compete on the European Tour were two very different things.

One day, while on vacation, Prodger met another caddie who mentioned that Nick Faldo needed someone to carry his clubs. Prodger met Faldo and worked one tournament with him, and the next week Faldo won the European PGA with Prodger on the bag. There was no looking back after that.

Prodger's was a nomadic career if ever there was one. After two successful years with Faldo, Prodger moved to the U.S. and worked for Chi Chi Rodriguez and a host of other players for brief periods. In 1983, he carried the clubs for the legendary Gary Player at the U.S. Open in Oakmount. Prodger reconnected with Faldo in 1986 at a time when Faldo was just hitting stride. Together, they won the 1987 British Open at Muirfield, and two years later the Masters.

Prodger almost won another Masters with Craig Parry in 1992, but they lost to Fred Couples down the stretch on Sunday. Prodger later connected with Colin Montgomerie, who has earned the wrath of colleagues for his methods of hiring caddies. Montgomerie was accused of poaching Prodger from Phillip Price, and then in 2003, he fired Prodger to replace him with Steve Rawlinson who had been working with Stephen Leaney.

Prodger steered "Monty" to the Ryder Cup, and after being replaced by Rawlinson, Prodger hooked up with K.J. Choi in September 2003. The two have been a spectacular pair ever since, and Choi has steadily grown into one of the top golfers in the world. It's no coincidence his ascent has come with one of the finest caddies around. ∎

STEVE WILLIAMS

Tiger Woods

The caddying equivalent to winning the lottery is being asked to carry the clubs for Tiger Woods. New Zealander Steve Williams hit this jackpot in 1999, after nearly 20 years of caddying with some of the greatest names in the golf world.

Williams started carrying bags at age six while working on his own golf game, but by his early teens he discovered a greater passion for carrying clubs than playing the game. His first break came

"Although Tiger doesn't really spend much time on the range during tournaments, he'll let me know what he has been working on, and it's my job to make sure that he is swinging in the way he wants to."

Steve Williams, shortly after being hired by Tiger Woods.

in 1976 when his father managed to get young Steve the job of caddying for Peter Thomson at the New Zealand Open, and Thomson hired him for tournaments whenever he played in that country. By the time Williams was 16, he had quit school and moved to Europe to caddy on that Tour.

Working most pro tours around the world, Williams earned an impressive reputation and in 1982 was offered the chance to work with Greg Norman. This was a part-time relationship until 1988 when Williams moved to the U.S. to work for Norman full-time, but just a year later Norman fired him.

Raymond Floyd immediately hired Williams and the two were a great pair for seven years until fate handed Williams the aforementioned lottery ticket. Woods had just fired Fluff Cowan, his first and only previous caddy. Tiger asked Floyd for permission to talk to Williams, and when the two met they hit it off and have been together ever since.

More than just carrying the bags, though, Woods and Williams have been a great team and have become friends. In the case of the former, there was a famous moment at the 1999 PGA Championship. On the 17th hole of a tense final day, Woods asked Williams for advice on a putt. "Inside left," Williams stated confidently. "You sure?" asked Tiger. Williams nodded. Tiger sank the putt, won the tournament, and sent Williams a framed photo with the note, "Great read on 17!" Woods and his wife Elin attended Williams's wedding, and the two couples spent a week together in New Zealand, having fun off the course.

Tiger believes that without Williams he wouldn't be as successful as he has been. A caddy can receive no greater praise than that. ■

GLOSSARY

ace a hole-in-one

address move beside the ball to prepare to hit it

albatross getting the ball in the hole in two shots on a par 5

all square both players in match play have won the same number of holes

approach shot a shot from the fairway to the green

attack (the flag) play an aggressive shot from the fairway, aiming for the pin, rather than an area of the green

away a player whose turn it is to take the next shot ("you're away")

back nine the last nine holes of a course

birdie one shot under par for a hole

bite backspin

bogey one shot above par for a hole

break the direction of a ball when putted on the green

bunker see sand trap

caddie a person who carries the clubs and bag of a player

Canadian Open the most important tournament in Canada

center cup a putt that goes into the middle of the cup (i.e., a perfect putt)

chip shot a short shot from the longer grass surrounding the green

claret jug a nickname for the trophy given annually to the winner of the British Open

club face the part of the golf club that makes contact with the ball

club head the part of the golf club that is attached to the shaft

clubhouse an area where golfers dress, relax, and eat meals

club selection a decision made between golfer and caddy to choose the correct club based on the ball's position to the flag

cut line the score after two rounds of golf (usu. Friday) that determines which players will play in the third and fourth rounds (usu. Saturday and Sunday) and which will not

divot the piece of turf lifted out of the ground during a shot

dogleg a hole which features a radical change in direction either left or right, about halfway between the tee box and the green

draw a shot which moves left to right (for a right-handed golfer)

driver a long-shafted golf club used to hit the ball a long distance, usu. from the tee box

drop a free lift and placement of the ball, usu. because of an impossible lie created by the course (e.g., water sprinkler) rather than the golfer

driving range a practice area where golfers can work on their shots and swing

eagle two shots under par for a hole

fade a shot which moves left to right (for a right-handed golfer)

fairway the long, narrow area straight ahead between the tee box and the green; the grass is kept short on the fairway

field the players entered in a specific tournament ("The field is always strong for the Canadian Open.")

final round the last 18 holes of any tournament

follow-through continuing the swing after hitting the ball

fourball a match-play event in which the best of two players' shots is used each time against the best shot of the two opponents

Friday the second day of most tournaments

front nine the first nine holes of a course

gimme a putt so easy it should be made successfully every time

Grand Slam the winning of each of the four major golf tournaments in a player's career (see major)

green see putting green

green jacket the jacket awarded annually to the winner of the Masters tournament

hacker a player lacking in skill

halve tie a hole in match play (i.e., take the same number of shots as an opponent)

handicap the number representing the average number of strokes above par a player expects to shoot over the course of 18 holes

hazard any area that is either off limits (water) or poses serious problems for a golfer (e.g., trees, thick rough)

heel the part of a club face closest to the shaft

honor a player who shoots first off the tee, usu. as a result of low score on the previous hole ("You have the honor on this hole.")

hook a ball that travels wildly in the same direction as the follow-through of a swing

in the final nine holes of a course (as opposed to "out")

in the black a score above par

in the red a score below par

iron a club made of this substance, ranging from a 1-iron to a 9-iron, used mostly as a second shot or on the tee of a par-3 hole

layup the second shot on a par-5 hole in which the player does not try to advance the ball directly to the green, but chooses to play to the fairway straight ahead, usu. about 100 yards from the green

leaderboard the scoreboard, mechanical or electronic, showing the leaders during a tournament

lie the position of the ball on the ground ("He doesn't have a very good lie in the high rough.")

line the direction the ball will travel along the green on the way to the hole

line up examine a putt to determine its direction on the way to the hole